D1603385

LEARN TO
LOVE
THE
TURBULENCE

LEARN TO
LOVE
THE
TURBULENCE

"Flight lessons" on becoming the
pilot in command of your own journey

BY AROUND-THE-WORLD PILOT
AMELIA ROSE EARHART
with KRISTIN CLARK TAYLOR

Pilot Pages LLC, Austin

ISBN 979-8-218-23396-9 (paperback)
ISBN 979-8-218-23397-6 (ebook)

Cover and interior design by John Lotte

Manufactured in the United States of America
First Edition

To my Mom, Debbie, from whom I got my wings and my Dad, Glen, my strong landing gear came from you.

TABLE OF CONTENTS

PREFACE

Prepare for headwinds.
Navigate with intention.
Brace for turbulence.
And with practice, even . . . *Learn to love the turbulence.*

These are not just empty aviation metaphors. They are living principles that are practiced in turbulent storms and critical phases of flight. These are the principles that I discovered and tested during my flight around the world, and now I want to offer them to you as we take off together toward this rarefied air. They also represent a few of the "flight lessons" we will explore as we navigate this book together.

I know they will resonate. Let them pick you up and lift you right off the page, because this book will teach you that the world is yours to fly. They describe so much of what I've done in my own life, both in the skies and on the ground—not just as a pilot but as a person. If you refer to the Table of Contents, you'll also see that these phrases serve as several of the chapter titles. Why? Because these are more than mere words. These are more than just flight lessons. These are *life lessons* that are carefully and purposefully woven throughout the fabric of every single chapter of this book.

While they represent my own bold, adventurous, and intentional life trajectory, I also offer them as a boarding pass to you: you, too, can upgrade yourself to pilot in command. You'll discover that there's an art to learning how to navigate the holding pattern. You will know your emergency

x   procedures and you'll learn to love the turbulence. These are only a few of the life lessons that will be fearlessly explored and boldly embraced with an openness and vulnerability that reflects the woman and the pilot I am today. This, dear reader, is the journey that we will actively navigate together as a flight crew.

So, climb into the cockpit with me. Strap in. And as we prepare for takeoff, as you line up on your runway, pressing the throttle forward to fly, your perspective will be elevated and expanded because this is what flight does: it changes your perspective by granting you permission to enter new airspace, both literally and figuratively.

The significance of sixteen

No one had ever flown around the world in the single-engine Pilatus PC-12 NG until I did it in 2014. As you can see from my equatorial flight path, I charted my course and completed this around-the-world journey in sixteen legs, with my copilot Shane Jordan sitting right seat as my partner. This is precisely why the book you are holding in your hands consists of sixteen chapters, one for each leg of that flight.

My hope is that by the time you've read the last chapter and we've touched down on that sixteenth runway, you will feel not just a sense of victorious, full-circle completion but will have also developed within you something powerful that I call *vision beyond sight* (also a Flight Lesson in this book). This is a book that is as much about discovery, self-awareness, fearlessness, and vulnerability as it is about attempting and completing a circumnavigation of the globe. I would describe it as a beautiful balance of both.

Before we take off together, let us take a clear look at
what's ahead of us on the horizon. Just as each pilot delivers
a complete preflight briefing before each takeoff, I want to
brief you on what kind of book you are about to read.

This isn't a book about the aviation industry or the history of aviation. This also is not a book that will teach you
how to fly. The Flight Lessons I share within these pages are
about life and living. Hopefully, they are lessons you will
take along with you on your journey as pilot in command of
your life. If you are interested in or are already taking that
bold step of learning how to fly, head to my website www.
AmeliaRoseEarhart.com to check out scholarship, training,
and career resources.

Though I will certainly draw from the depths (and the
heights) of my own firsthand experiences, you will not feel
a sequenced, narrative trajectory. Each chapter is a carefully
packaged, self-contained Flight Lesson unto itself. It is my
hope that as you read, the threads of each chapter will begin
to weave themselves into larger themes about life and living
in a way that touches your heart and heightens your awareness about how to navigate all kinds of life's unexpected
storms.

This is not a history book about the more famous Amelia
Mary Earhart. Links to historical information about Amelia
are on my website. My flight around the world, the opportunities granted through the Fly With Amelia Foundation, and
this very book were all created in honor of her memory, her
fierce trail-blazing actions, her tenacious spirit, and the bold
steps she took to define and advance aviation in every part
of the world, particularly for women. The reason she flew,
in her own words, was "to have this wonderful gift produce
practical results for the future of commercial flying and for

the women who may want to fly tomorrow's planes." I want to honor that vision.

This *is* a book that celebrates the joy that comes from learning to love the turbulence of life—the fits and starts, the bumpy encounters, the unexpected twists, turns, and disappointments—simply because this is sometimes what happens in life. I've always said that the only plane that never experiences turbulence is the one that stays locked up in the hangar. We don't want to stay locked in and locked down. Just as the Pilatus PC-12 NG was built to soar, we, too, are here to explore our own flight paths and to embrace the turbulence, the aborted takeoffs, the emergency landings. We will learn from *all* of it because nobody wants to fly with a pilot who has only flown through blue skies.

This is also a book that teaches us how to approach our goals—especially the major ones—one single step at a time. *One leg at a time.* This is the only way I could have planned—and completed—an around-the-world flight. My first step was to begin building a team, which eventually included more than one hundred people from all facets of aviation from all around the globe. Each leg of that flight was necessary to reach the next runway, just as each step of your journey will lead to new challenges and new joys. Yet, put together as a single entity—when all those legs became one single journey—they placed me on a trajectory that allowed me to circle the earth. My book celebrates this one-step-at-a-time, one-*leg*-at-a-time approach to life and living; together, we will celebrate its elegant simplicity and its powerful, practical sensibility.

To the future pilots holding this book in your hands right now, I want you to know that the world is yours to fly. I tell this to young women in aviation all the time—and now I'm sharing it with you. The world of flight does indeed belong to all of us, but it is especially important to me that as you consider a career in aviation, you hold this piece of truth particularly close to your heart. I hope this book serves as a compass that leads you to discover your direction, be it your true north or wherever your ever-changing path takes you.

To these young women, let me also say this: *I get you.* I didn't know where my flight path was going to take me when I was where you are now but know that you are welcomed here. This book is for you. Be encouraged, elevated, and uplifted by the lessons and the wisdom that I share. Realize that as you chart your course and make your decisions about life and living, nothing binds you, not even gravity.

While flying is a science, the act of flight has unlocked access to some magical places. Up there, I move above the earth, far above the complicated mindsets and the hang-ups that threaten to slow me down here on the ground; I even elevate beyond myself. Flight elevates my awareness and helps me relate to the world around me.

The beauty of this book is that it will not just chronicle *my* journey . . . it will invite you to explore, expand, and even redefine your *own*.

This book represents a new phase of flight for me, and I'm honored you've made the decision to join me.

So, let's go. Let's begin together by clearing ourselves for takeoff.

ACKNOWLEDGMENTS

To Amelia Mary Earhart, for living a tenacious life.

To her entire Earhart family everywhere, thank you for showing me grace as I grew (and continue to grow) into sharing this beautiful name. To the town of Atchison, Kansas, Amelia's hometown, thank you for the incredible tailwinds you have provided to the Fly with Amelia Foundation. With special thanks to Jacque and Clark Pregont, as well as the Atchison Chamber of Commerce.

To my around-the-world copilot, Shane Jordan. I hope you hear much of what you taught me in flight in these lessons.

To our team of dedicated partners and sponsors who made this flight possible: Pilatus Aircraft Ltd., Pratt & Whitney Canada, Honeywell Aerospace, BendixKing, Jeppesen, Inmarsat, Satcom Direct, Dallas Airmotive, Signature Flight Support, Lockton, Global Aerospace, 1st Source Bank, Survival Systems USA, Life Support International, Rimowa, GoPro, Canada Goose, Target, Oakley, and Wings Over the Rockies Air & Space Museum. Special thanks to Tom Aniello, Aaron DeBuhr, Jed Johnson, Nicole MacMillan, Phil Winters, Mike Beazley, Colleen Mahoney, Farzana Scofield, Thomas Bosshard, Teddy Spichtig, Denis Parisien, Mark Van Tine, Rhonda Larance, David McGowan, Jason Fish, Brian Keith, Matt York, Jeff Gayon, Dave Dickerson, Greg Anderson, John Barry, Barry Brown, Douglas Hardy, Ian Widmer, Sean Siff, Ian Cheyne, Katie Gerber, Patrick Carter, and beyond.

To my flight crew of Tom Nelson, Jillian Abramson and the entire Abramson Family, Raffael Marty, Sean Cavan, Jimmy Negri, Sheldon Senek, Haley Yax, Kathy Walker, Mark Cornetta, Lauren Chisholm, Marty Coniglio, Danielle xvi Grant, John Gillespie, Kelli McNeil, and Orly Orlyson . . . my dreams are reality because of your encouragement.

To my Mom, Debbie, and my Dad, Glen, this story exists because of you two! Thank you to my stepmother, Claudia Smith, my Grandma Aggie, and my cousin Jessica Benson. To my entire family, I love you.

I want to share a heartfelt thank you to everyone who generously donated to the Fly with Amelia Foundation, followed our journey on social media, and cheered us on along in flight.

Thank you to my sister scribe, Kristin Clark Taylor, for demanding I fully release and surrender while writing this book, which has proven to be my most meaningful accomplishment yet.

And finally, thank you, turbulence. In all your forms—past, present, and future.

MY FLIGHT AROUND THE WORLD

Departure date:	June 26, 2014
Return date:	July 11, 2014
Total number of miles:	24,385 nm
Total number of days:	18
Total number of legs:	16
Total number of countries:	14

	Number of nautical miles
1st Leg: June 26	
Oakland, California, to Broomfield, Colorado	814 nm
2nd Leg: June 27	
Broomfield, Colorado, to Miami, Florida	1,507 nm
3rd Leg: June 28	
Miami, Florida, to Trinidad and Tobago	1,396 nm
4th Leg: June 29	
Trinidad and Tobago to Natal, Brazil	1,857 nm
5th Leg: June 30	
Natal, Brazil, to Dakar, Senegal	1,623 nm
6th Leg: July 1	
Dakar, Senegal, to Sao Tome	1,674 nm
7th Leg: July 2	
Sao Tome to Tanzania	1,782 nm
8th Leg: July 3	
Tanzania to Seychelles	1,181 nm
9th Leg: July 3	
Seychelles to Maldives	1,205 nm

July 4 —Planned rest day

	Number of nautical miles
10th Leg: July 5	
Maldives to Singapore	1,828 nm
11th Leg: July 6	
Singapore to Darwin, Australia	1,808 nm
July 7—Planned rest day	
12th Leg: July 8	
Darwin, Australia, to Lae, Papua New Guinea	1,016 nm
13th Leg: July 9	
Lae, Papua New Guinea, to Bonriki, South Tarawa	
	1,663 nm
14th Leg: July 10	
Bonriki, South Tarawa, to Banana, Kiribati	1,783 nm
Crossing of the International Date Line— *Reason for July 10 showing up twice*	
15th Leg: July 10	
Banana, Kiribati, to Honolulu, Hawaii	1,155 nm
16th Leg: July 11	
Honolulu, Hawaii, to Oakland, California	2,093 nm

LEARN TO
LOVE
THE
TURBULENCE

1

CLEAR YOURSELF FOR TAKEOFF

LONG BEFORE my flight around the world was anything more than a wild daydream, I began flying in the same place all pilots do. On the ground. Specifically in ground school, learning the fundamentals of flight in a windowless class-room that felt oceans away from the blue-skies flying fan-tasies I'd been envisioning. Quickly realizing I would only be cleared for takeoff once I fully understood the process, I made it my personal habit, inside and out of the cockpit, to show up as if I'd *already* been cleared for takeoff.

4   The first step toward all of my aviation goals was for me to earn my pilot's license. Yes, I'd allowed myself mental and emotional clearance to learn how to fly, but without a pilot's license, I wasn't going anywhere. My point is this: Throughout life, we must give—and get—various forms of permission and acceptance to achieve our goals. It is a necessary step in the process of living . . . and certainly in flying.

The day I took my test to become a licensed private pilot

My designated pilot examiner was a long-time FAA employee who came highly recommended, known for being focused and fair. His ease around the plane made it seem like he'd given thousands of check rides through the years. No-nonsense and confident, he didn't make me feel like I was flying under a microscope, but I knew he was acutely aware of where my focus lay. Confirming I'd checked off the major boxes of understanding, he began to watch not just what I did but how I did it.

Mentor pilots had warned me that he wasn't likely to miss even the slightest detail, so I reminded myself to remain hyperaware of my movements while pre-flighting the Cessna 172. Each tire pressure check, radio frequency input, and communication with ground control had to be purposeful and precise. At any level of training, a check ride is a sacred, stressful flight for pilots, carefully prepared for and somberly regarded as the hour during which we prove our ability and professionalism in flight. If at any point I showed a lack of confidence or indicated in any way that I felt overwhelmed or if I failed to respond correctly to a command from air traffic control, the check ride could have ended immediately.

Weather conditions in LA were on my side that day in February of 2010. The forecast called for light, breezy winds with temperatures in the mid-sixties, which made my check-ride skies feel inviting.

The late afternoon sun would soon begin its slow descent; the blood-orange backdrop was segmented into triangles by crisscrossing trails left behind by other pilots who had recently flown in my airspace. Sitting in the left seat of the cramped cockpit, my examiner sat silently taking notes as I primed the engine, scanned my instruments, and prepared to turn the key. As I opened my door, the cool air hit my face, bringing me back to the excitement of the present moment and I smiled widely, confidently yelling, "Clear!" before turning the key, starting my engine for the very last time as a student pilot.

It had already been a very long day. *All* of my days were very long days, because that's how I thrive. Before my two-to three-hour-long afternoon flight lessons, my workday began with a three a.m. alarm buzzing me awake to head up above LA as an on-air reporter and airborne camera operator at Angel City Air, reporting daily on KCBS-TV and KCAL-TV. My "office" was a cobalt blue Eurocopter AS350 helicopter based at Whiteman Airport in Pacoima, California. I found instructors and training aircraft I could access both there and at Van Nuys Airport several miles down the road.

Between the hours I spent covering breaking news, high-speed LA car chases, wildfires, and even celebrity sightings from the chopper during the morning rush and the hours I spent flying as a student pilot in various rented Cessna 172s, there were days when I actually spent more time in the air

6 than on the ground. To put it simply, aviation had become my life. If you were to add up the number of *mental* hours I spent up in the sky—repeating emergency checklists to pass periodic phase checks, rehearsing the specifics of a complicated aerial maneuver, or planning how to intelligently cover an aerial news event at work—I was up in the sky twenty-four hours a day.

The day of my check ride, I experienced a healthy (but not overwhelming) dose of anxiety, as anyone prepping for an important professional exam would. My *mind* was the instrument I chose to focus on in this moment rather than my body, which was tense and unsettled from the worry. The skills I had developed and the attention I'd paid to truly understanding the concepts all meant that I'd already cleared *myself* for takeoff. As a confident and informed pilot, I had granted myself permission to proceed into new airspace, no longer as a student pilot but rather as a fellow aviator with whom my examiner would feel safe sharing the skies. Being in this mental headspace boosted my confidence and bolstered my desire to pass this test and become a licensed pilot. Attitude is everything.

That afternoon, I passed my check ride. Our hour-long flight was followed by a brief, informal chat, just the two of us, in an open hangar as the sunset blazed red above the valley. He gave me concrete advice about what I should pay attention to, weaknesses he picked up on in me that I could strengthen as a pilot. Then he signed my logbook, granting me the official FAA clearance I needed to take off into the world of flight as a certified, licensed pilot.

Quietly walking off the airfield toward my car, I felt an undeniable sensation of lift, as if an imaginary string were tugging me upward, back to the aerial paths I'd flown through the clouds. I had just entered new airspace . . . and I was already longing to return.

This first Flight Lesson, Clear Yourself for Takeoff, is intentionally chosen as the starting point for our sixteen-leg journey. Like the smooth asphalt runways from which aircraft take flight, this foundational lesson is the one I have discovered precedes all that follow.

Before we deserve to be given clearance to take off down any runway—and by this I mean invited to contribute to anything that requires us to step up, go all in, be a part of an elite or special community in any sense of the word—we maintain the best chance for staying in flight when we show up *in the know* and *ready to go*.

My flight instructor and dear friend, Sean Cavan, who instilled this high standard of preparation from day one of my commercial flight training, demanded I show up as a commercial pilot long before I received my license. Sean taught me that professional pilots only call the tower and request clearance to depart when they personally know and believe they are ready to take to the skies. The control tower may hear you *say* you're ready to go, but if you're searching for your flight charts, scribbling down critical instructions, and figuring things out as you go along, who's at fault when these distractions result in a crash?

It's certainly not the control tower who cleared you for takeoff.

It's the pilot.

Sean required me to write down my request for takeoff and say it aloud several times, to make sure I understood the meaning of the words, to become familiar with saying them and, to show that I was, in fact, deserving of operating a machine in the sky. Busy airspace requires pilots who are cleared

8 for takeoff to act with confidence, competence, and a clear understanding of where they intend to fly. No one was going to pay for my flight lessons or hold up flashcards in front of my tired eyes to help me memorize radio frequencies and emergency codes. This kind of preparation, purpose, and confidence had to come from within.

Before we can be cleared for takeoff—I'm talking that all-in, do-whatever-it-takes mindset—we must begin by committing to clearing oneself for takeoff toward each new goal, skill, or life change. When we commit, we know what it takes to accomplish what we want. And hey, if we don't, there's a vast network of experts always sharing their knowledge on the internet.

Just like I had flown that check ride thousands of times in my mind, I'd also circled around the world thousands of times, in my head, long before launching my actual flight around the world. This mental preparation, at times spent wandering through daydream loops of possibility, at other times focused on facts and figures, also taught me to control the rate of my ascent, and it bolstered my on-the-ground confidence, both in and out of aviation. *Attitude and mindset matter.* So, put in the mental work and show up prepared.

The talk

You've probably already lived enough of your life to know that in order to achieve any goal, in order to push past the limits and boundaries of your own expectations, you master the art of "the talk." By that, I mean that you must hone your ability to communicate clearly and advance your own directives in a way that other people can quickly and easily absorb.

Let me put it another way: Speak in a way that people understand. Be simple, direct, and succinct. Communicate your desires, your intentions, your hopes, your dreams, your potential flight plans, and your one-day-I'm-going-to-achieve-this goals with unapologetic precision. If you don't, you'll be left behind, shunted aside or kicked to the end of the line.

As I radioed into the control tower that day to receive clearance for takeoff, I had to assume the role of pilot in command. What is interesting is that the people in the tower don't know or care (and *shouldn't* know or care) whether the requesting pilot has been flying for decades or, like me, was taking her check flight to become a licensed pilot. At smaller airports, this may not be the case, but I was about to take flight into some of the busiest airspace in all of general aviation.

The only thing that matters is that you're about to be in the air and you better be prepared. If you don't jump in and say precisely (and immediately) what needs to be said to request clearance from the control tower, the controller will cut you off and make you wait, while other pilots on the runway who *are* prepared and who *do* know how to "get it done" move ahead of you.

I remember hearing the voices of all the other pilots in my headset who were requesting clearance for takeoff—all those male voices (I didn't hear one female voice, other than my own)—speaking to the tower in a calm, measured monotone that spoke to their professionalism as much as it did to their precision. I also remember thinking, *I've got to get in there, say what I need to say, and assert myself in a way that shows I mean it.*

Lined up and waiting ahead of and behind me were jets and airliners of every size. I knew, at that moment, that if

10   I didn't jump right in and speak, I wasn't being the most effective pilot I could be, which is never an acceptable option. So, I pressed my thumb down on the button, gave my coordinates, and proposed flight path, and requested my clearance for takeoff.

I got it, too.

The airspace surrounding Van Nuys Airport—in fact, most of the airspace in Southern California—is some of the busiest in the world for general aviation. So is the airspace around Centennial Airport in Denver, where I also did lots of flying and training. I am certain that having trained at these busy airports and learned the value of such precise communication benefited my professional life greatly, not just as a pilot, obviously, but as a television reporter and a public speaker today. Especially in high-stress situations, such precision can be a powerful tool.

I say all that to stress this: On a far more expansive scale, you have to know what your goals are before you can even think about communicating them clearly. You must know where you're going, how you're going to get there, and what your proposed flight path is going to look like. Before you can be cleared to take off toward *any* new goal, know what is required of you.

Listen up: knowing what you need and knowing how to *ask* for what you need are two separate and distinct skill sets. *Develop both.* If you don't, you'll end up stuck, pushed back, put on hold, forced to hang out in the hangar (or in a holding pattern), and waiting passively and patiently for clearance that might not ever come. *You can decide not to let this happen.* You can decide that you want, need, and deserve clearance to proceed. In the end (and in the beginning, too, I suppose) it really all rests with you.

My name is Amelia Rose Earhart 11

I'll never forget the moment of takeoff that afternoon. I'll always remember pushing forward on the throttle, feeling the nose rise slowly, slowly, my rented Cessna 172 straining to break free of the earth and pull up into the clouds. For those first few seconds, as the wheels of the plane roll faster, feeling lighter and lighter, eventually separating from the asphalt below, you can almost *feel* the plane wanting to take flight, seemingly longing to break away from the earth (it's called "ground effect," which we'll examine in an upcoming chapter). Ground effect only lasts for about fifteen seconds, but within those fifteen seconds is something infinite and exhilarating: Potential. Transformation. Energy. The excitement that comes from pulling away from one space (the earth) and elevating to the next (the sky). There are boundless possibilities that exist within that tiny, transformative, sacred space.

In this critical decision-making moment, the aircraft has both the potential to fall back to the ground or the potential to take flight—it all depends on which control input the pilot decides to use. Pull the nose up, inch the yoke back toward your ribcage, and you generate lift to fly. Push the nose down, on the other hand, just a fraction of an inch, and all momentum is lost, sending you back to the ground, where you will roll to a stop.

As I rose into the February sky that Friday afternoon, every cell in my body felt uniquely alive, humming with energy. I could feel the beating of my heart and the pounding of my pulse; I could even feel my brain reminding me not to hold my breath. I was also vitally aware that just a few thousand feet beneath me, bolted to solid ground, was the seven-foot-tall bronze statue of Amelia Mary Earhart, standing proud in her baggy pants and rumpled flight jacket, sending me on my way. At the time of her disappearance, Amelia and her husband, George Putnam, lived in North Hollywood, and in 1980, the community raised close to $20,000 to complete her likeness, so she was standing just below me when I made my flight, ushering me forward and upward.

With one Amelia flying overhead and the other anchored to the earth below, a small smirk crept across my face as I allowed this beautiful coincidence to sink in. With a whispered "Thank you," I marked a private and necessary acknowledgement of just how tenacious both of our flight goals were, each in their own way. I became suddenly aware of a new sensation that *this* Amelia *Rose* Earhart was qualified and prepared to fly the aircraft. Rather than spending my flight hours obediently tracking her shadow in the sky, I gave myself permission to fly a heading that was mine and mine alone. I'd propel my aircraft toward a chosen purpose under my own power, allowing the spontaneous times when my path crossed Amelia Mary's to serve as gentle reminders that unlike the requirements to obtain a pilot's license, there were no tests I needed to pass to feel connected to this woman after whom I was named. That type of meaning could only be given or taken away by me.

There have been many times in my life Amelia has shown up along my path . . . or maybe I've shown up along hers. Each time we find one another, be it through a movie reference, a physical location, or a shared Amelia story from a stranger, these moments tend to feel more like nods from the universe letting us know it is okay to fly different paths. It's like a friend who you may only check in with a few times a year, *but when you do,* you pick up right where you left off before, without missing a beat.

My check ride had to be complete by twilight, which meant it would be time to land soon. Gazing down at the stretch of red brake lights seemingly painted on the 405 freeway, it reminded me of lava—not just the color but the pace at which it was moving—and it almost reminded me that I wanted to stay as far away from those brake lights on the ground as I possibly could. It hit me then: clearing myself for takeoff toward less crowded airspace would become a way of life from here on out.

Not only did this newly elevated and expanded perspective shift how I approached flight, it also led me to relate to my career as an airborne television traffic reporter in a more meaningful way, through reporting real-time solutions and alternate routes to help drivers regain even a fraction of their precious time.

The decisive moments of the check ride were quickly approaching. Soon I'd be contacting the control tower, requesting permission to land, and reviewing my final-approach checklist, and as I mentally reviewed which skills I had left to demonstrate, I felt confident that I'd passed my check ride. My examiner remained focused of my every move, but that didn't stop me from taking a few seconds up there to smile in appreciation at the unusual set of circumstances that had led me to this moment—and it goes all the way back to my parents, Debbie Dale and Glen Earhart.

When my mom was pregnant with me, my parents had quite different ideas about the pros and cons of naming me Amelia. One view was that such a famous name would create too much baggage that might weigh me down, while another view was that the name would inspire optimistic "what ifs"

14   that might lead to aviation career choices and adventurous hobbies. Like every parent, both my mom and dad wanted to ensure that I had all the opportunities they never did.

Through the years, my understanding of the reason behind why my parents named me Amelia Earhart has fallen somewhere between parents' good intentions and what our Earhart side of the family had been told was a distant common ancestry shared with the original Earhart family tree. When I was born in 1983, online genealogical searches were still about two decades away from being commonplace, so if your grandparents shared stories about your family tree, you had no reason to question them. The timing of my birth, the creation of the internet, and improved access to public records, all factor in when I put myself in my parents' position as they grappled with the decision.

While attending college, I saved up my tips from waitressing to invest in genealogical research that could, once and for all, answer the question of how I was related to the famous pilot. While the genealogist described her process of linking together what she called a "likely distant biological relationship," she went on to tell me that the exact relation could only be determined and revealed after an additional investment of several thousand more dollars, due to the complexity of the European record-keeping process. At the end of this search, I felt somewhat relieved, and while I couldn't afford to pay for the full report, I had at least established the connection. But rather than my family expressing gratitude at learning of the connection, their reaction felt more like "Well, of *course* we're related to Amelia Earhart; we told you that all along." In hindsight, confirmation bias, defined by *Encyclopedia Britannica* as the "tendency to process information by looking for, or interpreting, information

that is consistent with one's existing beliefs," played a key
role in how I viewed identity, which we'll explore further in
upcoming chapters.

At the heart of it all, I now know that who we *choose* to
relate to says far more about our character than to whom we
are related.

Clear your ideas for takeoff

A week doesn't go by where I don't get asked the question, "How on earth did you plan a flight around the world?
Isn't that really complicated / dangerous / unnecessary / expen-
sive . . . ?" The list of reasons *not* to attempt a flight this complex could go on and on and on.

Just as we can prepare ourselves to show up to life's challenges equipped with an understanding of our subject, we
can also clear our most audacious ideas for takeoff without
waiting for permission from anyone else. In the earliest
stages of dreaming up my around-the-world flight, there was
no fancy airplane, no fuel or fuel tank, no flight crew hoping
for our safe arrival.

There was only a pilot equipped with a map and a ruler.

We'll dive into the details of my route and why I charted
the specific course I did in the next Flight Lesson, but long
before there were even logistics to consider and storms to
navigate around, the hardest work had just begun. The intan-
gible and amorphous (even to me) dream of a global flight
honoring Amelia had to be meticulously developed, grown
as a flexible plan, tested as a brand, sold as a concept, and finally accepted and remembered by those who consumed the
story as a success.

16   In order to begin clearing my idea of a flight around the world, I kept notebooks of my handwritten lists of all the reasons why my flight could fail. No, I wasn't stuck dwelling on the negative. Rather, I was slowly and meticulously researching the weaknesses within my own concepts, evaluating all the multiple perspectives so that I could remain flexible and realistic as the plan moved forward. Being exceedingly rigid about where, when, and how we would fly wouldn't get me around the world. The one thing we should never bend on is our commitment to remaining flexible when attempting audacious goals. Excessive rigidity has a way of clipping one's wings.

There was also another particularly important factor. Once I'd decided to go all in on this flight around the world, a new type of work became mandatory: raising enough capital to make it happen. This included building pitches for Fortune 500 companies, developing complex media kits, and thinking big-picture concepts one minute and filing a request for a special flight permit over the Congo the next. More than just raising the money, it also meant establishing trust with these corporations and instilling within them a sense of total confidence in this young pilot named Amelia Rose Earhart who wanted to fly around the world.

I didn't need to walk into each pitch meeting with all the answers but I needed to consistently show these companies that I was the one to complete this incredibly difficult, dangerous, and by most accounts, unnecessary flight around the world—and that they could trust me as the pilot in command, both in and out of the cockpit. This had as much to do with character as it did with competence.

When Pilatus Aircraft agreed to partner with me, it spurred momentum from other important partners and resources. With a global team assembled, we entered an agreement that had never been struck before in the history of aviation: We were on track to attempt the first-ever equatorial flight around the world in a Pilatus PC-12 NG. Additionally, no one had ever modified a Pilatus PC-12 NG. And to successfully complete this single-engine flight around the world, we needed to design, build, install, and test a 200-gallon auxiliary fuel tank inside a $4.5 million airplane.

Requesting permissions of this size and import meant I needed to show up prepared, not only in my understanding of their business but also in my actions, to prove I wasn't in search of a free ride. During the pitch meeting, the executives asked the very fundamental (and very fair) questions, "What do you know about our aircraft? Have you ever *flown* our Pilatus-12-NG before?"

I believe my answer helped seal the deal. "Yes," I answered with confidence, handing over my newly acquired Pilatus PC-12 NG endorsement from Flight Safety.

I had twenty-eight sponsors in all and I proudly share that I did not lose the partnership of even one of them along the way, a rare feat in and of itself.

There are several life lessons in all of this. The first is that you must be *obsessed* with achieving your goals. Be bold and audacious in your preparation to meet (and exceed) your goals—and the bigger the goal, the bolder you must be.

The silver lining

In 2014, I booked a one-way commercial flight from Denver to Switzerland. Why was there no return ticket home? I wouldn't need one, as I was about to fly N58NG, the

18 brand-new PC-12 from the Pilatus headquarters in Stans, Switzerland, back to Denver, Colorado. This was the first time I had ever traveled to Europe. Who would have ever guessed that my first flight to Europe would be to pick up a $4.5 million aircraft that I was going to use to fly around the world?

Before we flew the plane back to the United Sates, across the North Atlantic, only three hours had been logged on the engine to test the engine performance over the Swiss Alps before our North Atlantic crossing. The plane itself was elegant: a sleek, silver work of art that was poetry in motion. Almost immediately, I began calling the plane my *Silver Lining*, because the plain and simple truth is that that's exactly what it was. My silver lining.

For my ferry pilot Theodor Spichtig and me to deliver the plane to the Pilatus facility here in the United States, we would make required stops for fuel, food, and rest in Prestwick, Scotland; Reykjavik, Iceland; and Iqaluit, Canada, before finally completing our mission in Broomfield, Colorado. Touching down, I felt one with the plane. The North Atlantic crossing was rigorous and challenging, and I felt ready to learn everything I could make my journey come to life.

As we continue to line ourselves up along that solid white line in the middle of each new runway, the horizon stretched out before us, the wide-open sky ready to embrace us as we push our throttle forward, we must remember that *no* pilot has ever been led by the hand onto a runway and encouraged to take flight. This we must do for ourselves. No one else will do it for us.

No one was going to drag me toward planning, fundraising, training or completing a flight around the world. It took me waking up each day, and sometimes in a moment-by-moment progression throughout the day, to clear myself for takeoff.

I need to say this part again: *mindset matters.* Knowing what to ask for, when to ask for it, and how to state your terms is of paramount importance.

So, find your silver lining. And if you don't have one, *develop* one.

Clear yourself for takeoff. If you don't do it, no one else will.

Chart your own course. (The very next chapter will lift us up and fly us right toward it.)

But before we get there, let's end with this piece of essential knowledge: In your lifelong pursuit of new takeoffs and new journeys, let your enthusiasm and your commitment fuel your focus. Train your brain to become mentally pliable, resilient, and aware. Embrace the beauty of creativity along the way, even (perhaps *especially*) if you live in a world of uncompromising precision. I am living proof that these two things—uncompromising precision and the courage to be creative—can indeed coexist.

FLIGHT LESSON

2

CHART YOUR OWN COURSE

MY JOURNEY BECAME MY OWN only when I gave up trying to fly a straight line around a curved world.

In my experience, our authentic selves are eventually revealed one way or another, either by choice when we represent ourselves fully and speak up for what we want, or by force when we can no longer tolerate the compromise of losing ourselves along a path that we once agreed to follow. Charting your own course takes practice, but once you taste the freedom of forging your own path, you'll develop the skill of being—and constantly searching for—your very best self.

For me, the beauty of being my best self is found in the
transitions from life's imbalances and bumps back to smooth
flight, all the while flying through the turbulent skies with
the knowledge that turbulence, while it doesn't usually cause
crashes, serves us by jolting us back to the reality of the responsibility at hand. Yes, the bumps along the way can sometimes be disconcerting, disillusioning, and sometimes downright disorienting, but if we stay on course—or even if we
decide to change course, which will invariably be required at
some points—the absolute knowledge that it is *our course to
change* is what will keep us afloat, aloft, and intact.

I know that I must be bold in my pursuits, even when
I might feel meek. Brave in how I live my life, even when
I might feel frightened. Deeply rooted in my own identity,
this is what will allow me to soar. It is the beautiful balance
again: believe in yourself and your capabilities—even when
it feels safer to throw in the towel, take the path of least resistance, and buckle under the pressure and expectations
of others. Resist the urge. This course called life is yours to
chart. So, chart it with intention.

When we insist on following the path of others, we automatically set ourselves up for failure. Charting our own
course allows us to *own our own* journey—turbulence, delays,
hard landings, and all.

Kitchen table confidence

I spent two full years (from 2012 to 2014) planning my
around-the-world flight by putting pencil to paper, carefully building a comprehensive plan to not only demonstrate
how the logistics would all come together but to show that

22   such a journey would resonate with the rest of the world in a way that could make potential sponsors and partners proud. I knew going in that the feasibility of a weather-dependent, high-risk, international adventure of this kind was low. According to Earthrounders.com, as of 2020 the total number of successful single-engine, around-the-world flights sits at 238. To put it in an even wider perspective, NASA cites the number of total crewmembers on all 135 space shuttle missions at more than three times that number, 833. Put simply, I knew how special it was to attempt something so rare, so I took it seriously.

Looking back, I'm incredibly proud of my younger self, not just for having the guts to invite myself to join such an exclusive group but to do the work to make it in. Why? The world of aviation is surgical in its precision. It is exacting, unyielding, and razor-sharp in its focus and its consistency. At its core, at its essence, and standing at the very center of its foundation are figures, formulas, and flight plans that are unfaltering and unwavering. Nothing is left for interpretation. The boundaries are clear, as are the expectations, and I like it that way, most of the time.

This undertaking—combining the mechanics of flight and the human factor of connecting two Amelias seventy-seven years apart—was a challenge. The flight needed to be soft *and* strong, intentional, *and* open to interpretation, all complicated concepts to manage on any complex journey.

Factoring in the complexity of appropriately honoring the presence of one of history's most revered icons, I knew this flight would require me to push the boundaries of my creative mind and require enough honest self-reflection to trust that "all in" vote in my heart. I reminded myself often that "No one is making you do this flight," and "There is an actual chance you could die/be seriously injured/wreck the plane and embarrass yourself in front of the entire world/ hurt someone else." The list could have gone on and on and on . . . if I'd let it.

I could see the headlines in my mind. "Doomed Flight of Second Amelia Earhart Crashes in the South Pacific!" Talk about a social media heyday. I share this to give a little insight into the rabbit holes my mind would travel down when things began to feel a little overwhelming.

Sitting at my kitchen table in the rented apartment I'd chosen based on its proximity to my three-times-a-week instrument flight lessons at Centennial Airport, I grappled with the higher-level considerations involved with tackling such a tremendous project. With a basic world map, a ruler, and a calculator, I slowly and intentionally mapped the 1937 route of Amelia Mary Earhart.

When I'd drawn the first thirty legs of her and her navigator Fred Noonan's adventure on the map, including the three final, long stretches not flown following the crew's disappearance en route to Howland Island, I remember feeling more blown away by her bravery than I'd ever felt before. Looking at this brave and courageous path, how could I *not* be tempted to follow her route exactly?

Weighing the possibilities, the potential pitfalls, and the ultimate purpose of anything even close to a re-creation flight required scratching every idea and refusing to pass any judgment on myself—no matter how wild the questions of how, why, and where became. I kept sketching and I kept drawing things out. (More on this in the next chapter.)

Eventually, of course, these sketches and preliminary plans became a finely tuned blueprint for what the final flight would become, but these first napkin drawings, these first early steps, proved that even ideas of global proportions can begin in the simplest of moments.

Leaning back in my chair, I caught my reflection in the mirror across the room. For hours, I'd allowed my mind to soar in any direction I chose across those aeronautical charts; in those moments, I'd allowed *possibility* to take flight. Mounted behind me, as a backdrop to all this enthusiasm, was the large black-and-white framed image of Amelia Mary in flight over the Oakland Bridge in California.

If Amelia could stay true to herself, flying her own course, both on foot and in flight, back in the thirties, I owed it to myself (and to her) to do what was right for me. I would not let opinions from naysayers and critics who felt I needed to retrace her exact route play into my decision. I would disregard those who said that flying in anything other the same Lockheed Electra 10E-style plane Amelia flew would be "easy." Silencing the voices of the naysayers allowed me to hear my own voice more clearly.

Looking back, I now recognize the power and intensity of that single moment as I mentally detached from the self-imposed train tracks I'd locked myself onto that once dictated I fly along Amelia's *actual* path. I prioritized all the things that were important to me and to the ultimate success of this trip, placing safety, navigation, technology, and engine ability above the empty opinions of the critics and naysayers. In the end, seven of my landings matched up to Amelia's original route, but truthfully, I wasn't counting, because for me, she was along for the entire ride.

Flight as a work of art

More than anything else, I am creative. I am a bold, free thinker, and I am aware enough to know that such laser-like precision and unyielding adherence to rule-following will not satiate my free spirit. Rather than separate my passionate pursuits by physical walls, I let them coexist. If you were to peek into my home, the dichotomy would be clear: Paint brushes, canvases, and pieces of my own artwork fill the spaces of my sun-splashed art studio. A vintage propeller leans on the wall near my painter's easel. Flight logs and even the face of my auxiliary fuel tank switcher panel from my around-the-world flight are nestled in with the other keepsakes in my home, many of which have circled the globe with me.

The exacting nature of aviation requires the pilot to stay focused, constantly scanning instruments and monitoring the big picture. How does a creative like me keep from going crazy up there? All that focus, all the attention we've been trained to pay to following rules and abiding by regulations is rewarded with moments of ethereal beauty. These moments of beauty show up constantly, in a variety of forms from dust particles suspended in sunbeams, distinct white clouds edged against the flat, blue sky, and double rainbows emerging from thunderstorms at twilight. But these images don't belong to me alone. Even the toughest military pilots I know can't resist keeping an eye out for the exceptional sights.

This is probably why I never *fully* fit into the aviation world, and although I hold my Commercial Pilot's Certificate, I'm not interested in a traditional career in commercial aviation. I fly when I speak on stage and share my

26   story. I fly when I paint my aerial abstract works, and when I write these pages. In these ways, flying is and always will be a vital part of my personal and professional life.

Was there once a time when I felt like I was chasing Amelia? You bet. But today, the chase is finished. Why? *Because we have found each other.* I mentioned in the first chapter how she "shows up" in my life from time to time—as I was flying over her statue as I was taking my test to become a private pilot, for instance. These are not mystical, other worldly visits. She is simply put in my path when it is meant to happen, plain and simple. These are powerful, precious, and deeply personal encounters; and that they happen in the quiet, private space of my own daily life makes them even more meaningful to me.

Amelia has made her presence known at other times as well: when I first moved to LA to take a job as television helicopter reporter with Angel City Air, reporting on KCBS and KCAL-TV (in 2012), my new job was based at Whiteman Airport, and my apartment was in North Hollywood, just five minutes away. Well, Amelia came to visit me then—or more accurately, I'd come to visit *her.*

Here's what I wrote in my journal only days after I'd moved in: "As I looked out the window of my extravagantly sleek NoHo apartment, I saw the outline of a life-sized sculpture of a woman glowing and damp in the contrast of the yellow streetlight. The next morning, I remember having that butterflies-in-the-stomach feeling as I walked through the park, the familiar hum of a Cessna 172 engine calling my attention to the hazy morning skies overhead . . ."

The journal continues, but the gist of it is that as I arrived at the statue, I first looked up at the sky to see a Cessna 172 making its way through the clouds. I had not been up in a while, and as I watched the Cessna pushing across the sky, I said to myself, "Damn. I've got to get back up there."

When I pulled my gaze down from the sky and focused on reading the statue's plaque, it told me all I needed to know: *it was Amelia.*

I remember laughing aloud at the irony and the joy of it all. I laughed at the miraculous sight of that Cessna 172 zipping across the blue sky just above me; it was the very model I'd flown to get my pilot's license. I laughed at the fact that this extraordinary woman and aviation heroine was standing tall before me, inches away. I laughed at the fact that I had unknowingly leased my new apartment within eyesight of this woman who helped chart the course of my life trajectory.

I laughed.

"Blue skies, Amelia," I whispered under my breath.

These moments where she finds me tend to align with the times when I'm most enjoying the ride of my own flight, lost in the moment, just having fun. It happened—for the first time, actually—in 1998, when my mom remarried and we moved to tiny Tonganoxie, Kansas. Whether it was providence or coincidence I cannot say, but what I can say is this: our new home was only about ten miles from Atchison, Kansas, Amelia's birthplace. I was in high school at the time, and people there were, and are, very protective of Amelia's legacy (rightfully so), and even as a seventeen-year-old, I was understandably concerned about how they'd react to my presence.

I was still feeling shame for not knowing whether I was related to Amelia but the residents never made me feel unwelcome. Everyone made me feel welcome, and they still do to this day. Each year I attend the Amelia Earhart Festival, where in 2013, I was awarded the Pioneering Achievement

28 Award. I used that $10,000 award as the initial contribution to the Fly with Amelia Foundation (more on that later). From the beginning, I felt that these residents, more than most, understood the complex weight of carrying her name. This, I believe, also helped solidify my sense of self-identity. There, perhaps because I saw Amelia wherever I turned—in sculpture, in small-town street signs, in murals, even in a giant earthwork of her likeness in the Kansas cornfields near her childhood home—I blended in. For the first time, I saw the ways others had chosen to honor her life. The flight would be my way to quietly add to this collection of tributes.

In charting my own course, I didn't veer away from Amelia. I veered closer to her. Here we were, both simply women—with this woman (me) choosing to go her own way.

Air pressure

Admittedly, my around-the-world flight was a very "clickable" story: social media attention was high, the aviation community was watching closely, and my working as an on-air helicopter reporter heightened the interest in the journalistic community. People from all walks of life knew my face and my name. They were eager to follow the story, reaching out through heartfelt letters and emails, many sharing the qualities they loved most about Amelia.

I hope it resonates when I share that I didn't embark on the journey for attention or publicity. I embarked on the journey because I *wanted* to do it—for myself, for the young women who will fly in the skies with me (and after me) one day, to honor Amelia, and to quench this insatiable thirst to complete a circle around this planet.

Did I struggle with doubts and fears during that time? Of 29 course, I did. I still do. I'm human. But over the years, I have learned to respect my doubts and fears without *surrendering* to them. Instead, I own them as they surface—they are legitimate emotions, after all—but I don't remain stuck within them. Like a few harmless clouds passing through my airspace, I am aware of their presence, but I no longer stress and fret that these clouds will erupt into a towering thunderstorm. Learning how to chart my own course, not just in the context of my around-the-world journey but in how I live my life and go after my goals, helps elevate me to a higher level of self-acceptance and self-awareness of my fears and flaws. Sometimes this process is clumsy, but at the heart of this message is a gentleness with (and acceptance of) myself that reminds me to save room for patience and empathy for others navigating their own complicated and sometimes stormy routes.

The author Deepak Chopra says that a person who exhibits both positive and negative qualities, strengths, and weaknesses, "is not flawed, but complete."

I urge you, next time you're getting rocked by life's turbulence, during even a split-second break from the jolts and the bumps of the storm you're navigating, to remember that the pilot who has only flown through blue skies isn't lucky . . . she's inexperienced.

Charting a career course all my own

Long before I'd ever charted my own course in an airplane, I was bound and determined to use all directions on my personal compass. Jimmy Negri, one of my best friends to this

30   day, was my partner in flight when I worked in a traffic-reporting position flying on the 50,000-watt talk radio station, NewsRadio 850 KOA. As the radio reporter, I sat in the backseat as Jimmy flew from the front right seat, with a TV reporter operating the camera from the front left.

Jimmy, a former Denver police helicopter pilot with thousands of hours of flight experience, flew what he called our "three-million-dollar office" with the casual comfort and confidence of a teenage boy navigating his bike around the block of his childhood home. Having grown up in Denver, he knew every nook and cranny, every block and boulevard, of the city. "Safe" is an understatement for how I felt up there with Jimmy at the controls, not just because of his familiarity with the countless cross streets and obscure locations we covered but, even more importantly, because of his awareness and understanding of the sophisticated and nuanced communication required to be the best at what he did. And, of course, above all, were his superb piloting skills.

Jimmy and I were an award-winning team, and we complemented each other perfectly; he piloted the helicopter, and I covered the news, both as a reporter and a camera operator. We spent a total of four years, equating to thousands of hours together in the air, covering everything from a powerful tornado that touched down less than twenty-five miles away from the stadium that was then hosting the 2008 Democratic National Convention to the World Series as the only aircraft permitted over the stadium during play.

In a symbolic way, I consider Jimmy to be my first copilot. The trust between us was mutual and necessary. It still is today. While I never took control of the helicopter (I was there as a reporter), he never failed to treat me as an equal member of his flight crew, including me in the decision-making process whenever he could as we covered a story.

Before Jimmy and I became the dynamic duo of breaking news, the helicopter was an aerial resource not only for 850 KOA, but it was also used by KUSA-TV as a shared partnership, requiring two reporters and one pilot to get the job done. When the position of TV reporter and videographer opened up, I remember feeling incredibly protective of our professional, respectful, delicate ecosystem of workflow we had built up there. Sharing this with Jimmy, we walked into our flight-planning office and discussed the logistics of a possible solution.

What if I pitched a combination role of radio and TV reporting from the helicopter?

You don't simply pitch a brand-new role on a well-established news team at two of the top radio and TV stations in the country easily; a pitch of this kind was very unusual. I knew this, and so did Jimmy. Instead of dropping a casual email to see if management would want to think it over, I decided to sit down and create the plan, carefully evaluating it from every angle, trying to anticipate their questions before they could even ask them.

Without hesitation, Jimmy was ready to help me detail this plan; a plan that had many benefits because it would not only fill the station's open role but would also save both stations a significant amount of money by combining two roles into one. Before then, I had been the backup for the helicopter TV reporter who was relocating to another city, which meant I was already familiar with operating the complex camera and had built rapport with the journalists with whom I'd be working.

I went home and typed up the combination proposal.

32   I made the pitch to both management teams, breaking down all the benefits, equipped with Jimmy's supportive reasoning in my mental flight bag.

Creating this dual role was important to me for several reasons. One, it gave me the courage and confidence I needed to visualize something new, pitch the idea, and define it as I went, setting a standard that was only as high as I demanded it be. Two, this trusting partnership I had with Jimmy also represented the first time I remember feeling truly *supported* in a big idea; having a teammate there for assistance and encouragement while I took responsibility for the details of bringing it to life made all the difference in the world. Together, we made the idea airworthy.

On my very last day in my role as TV/radio reporter/photographer before moving to LA to take the helicopter reporting position Jimmy had insisted I go for, I brought my best friend and pilot in command a frame filled with some of our most meaningful memories, signed at the bottom with the note, "We made every day fun." I'd like to think that this gift I gave to Jimmy—both the framed memories and the note I wrote at the bottom—demonstrated our ability to not only chart our own course but to choose our attitude and mindset about that course with integrity and intention.

3

UPGRADE YOURSELF TO PILOT IN COMMAND

AT THE EARLY STAGES of writing this book, when I first sat down to develop the outline and identify the most important themes and lessons I wanted to include, "Pilot in Command" was what I'd named this Flight Lesson. Being the pilot in command of your own flight is an important theme, and it's one I speak and write about often. But something in me, even then, told me the title needed an intentional tweak, elevating this concept from a label to an action.

34   That's why I decided to insert the three additional words, *Upgrade Yourself to*, to emphasize that there is purposeful action involved in becoming pilot in command. When we upgrade ourselves, we give ourselves a permission slip for unlimited growth, on *our* terms. This represents a slight course correction—it is a deliberate decision and an intentional shift in perspective—and the moment you make it, you transition from being the passive, back-seat passenger on someone else's flight to being the pilot in the cockpit of your own plane.

In the process of planning the global trip, upgrading myself to pilot in command became priority number one as I walked into each new challenge. Trust me, if I hadn't pulled the throttle back on every aspect of moving this flight forward (between the overflight permits, visas, interviews, etc.), no one was going to do it for me. With this mindset, teamwork and collaboration became the powerful engine of the flight, and I loved adding the fuel of focused enthusiasm. In this Flight Lesson, I invite you to assume this position of authority in your own life, too.

I chose the word *upgrade* because in this Flight Lesson, we're raising our standards. Sure, riding as a passenger on someone else's flight can be comfortable; there's less risk involved. For example, staying in a career path that leaves us empty inside but still fills our bank account enough to tolerate the discomfort is what being a passenger can feel like. I'm not telling you to quit your job, but with the focus of someone who has personally upgraded herself to pilot in command in many ways, I can say it's worth it to take the controls, put in the effort, and allow yourself to fly in the rarified air I described in the book's introduction. This airspace is wide open and yours to fly.

Upgrading yourself to pilot in command is entirely possible. It starts with an honest personal assessment of the destination you're trying to reach, the amount of fuel on board your plane, and yes, the sacrifices you'll need to make to get there. Just as I couldn't load the plane with unnecessary cargo, you've got to pare down your load to what's essential, and once you've done that, you've got to *commit*. A pilot in command signs off on who and what is on board, and yes, this can also mean disappointing those who expected you to remain on board their flight.

But the moment you make that shift, perhaps deplaning a mission bound for a destination you know deep down isn't yours, you become a navigator. A navigator is someone who starts that new business, ends the relationship that has run its course, goes back to school after a long hiatus, takes up a new hobby, or learns a new language.

A navigator sits down and writes her book.

Regardless of how this theme and this Flight Lesson resonate in your own personal life, really let it sink in that this is an option that belongs to each one of us. It is not reserved just for the privileged few, the lucky, the naturally talented, or just for those who lead bold, audacious lives. It is waiting, as a viable option, *for all who choose it*. This choice lives only in the present moment, and you're the only one who has the key to unlock what's yet to come.

Risk is involved—and that's by design. When we have got something to lose, I believe we tend to naturally operate at a higher frequency; once we've assumed this all-in position, there are consequences with ripple effects of which we may not even be aware. Here's the trade-off: this new level of control means you are now also in full control of who gets to board your flight. You don't have to tolerate

36 disruptive, disrespectful, or destructive passengers. Revoke their boarding passes immediately, kindly, and directly. But hear me loud and clear: removing the expectations, opinions, shame, and all the other emotional and mental baggage that others have heaved onto your flight without your permission in the past can feel as exhilarating as taking off in an F-16. But you must do it yourself.

You'll learn quickly that a heightened situational and environmental awareness is key, especially through turbulent storms that will inevitably speckle your path. The beautiful tradeoff, of course, being that the higher we climb, the more perspective we acquire over our airspace and the more easily we can spot oncoming storms.

Upgrading yourself to pilot in command doesn't mean that you necessarily hold the title of boss or decision-maker or that you must show some other visible title of authority to the outside world. You can just as easily be pilot in command of your own, quiet, singular project that involves no one else but you. This is an empowering, exhilarating, and yes, a little intimidating way of thinking, acting, and being. It will give you newfound confidence that that will *propel* you on this journey that will, at times be turbulent, but will always be your own. You'll decide intentionally who to bring on board your flight, and you will be able to relate to and interact with others who understand and respect you, and you will enjoy the unexpected tailwinds that can come from finding just the right crew for your flight.

Go or no-go: the decision belongs to you

What I've shared so far are more than mere analogies and comfortable comparisons to the world of flight. These are principles that are actually *practiced* by pilots.

In the world of aviation, the pilot in command holds complete and total authority of every aspect of his or her flight at every, single moment. There is a concept in aviation aptly named the "go-no-go" decision, and it speaks to this very principle: when a pilot in command prepares for takeoff, he or she has weighed not only the risks and the hazards but also the *pressures* of taking flight. For example, a charter pilot may feel pressured to take off into hazardous weather conditions to deliver the passengers to an important business meeting. These pressures, while difficult to resist, must be met with clear boundaries that make safety the top priority.

The pilot alone can decide to abort takeoff, to declare an in-flight emergency, or even to perform a precautionary landing—*for whatever reason*. Yes, for straightforward mechanical issues, but also when something *feels* off and needs to be identified before pressing on.

Knowing full well there were far more reasons *not* to attempt this flight than to make that all-in, "go" decision, I took the responsibility for overcoming doubts by deciding what my limits were when it came to risks and hazards—but only after weighing facts with emotion. I made that critical mental transition from being a passenger sitting coach in the back row to realizing I was the only one who could make the go-no-go decision to take off on this flight as Amelia Rose Earhart.

So, I *did* it.

When flying as a crew, the physical shift to the left seat of the plane (where the pilot in command sits), while short

38   in distance, is a monumental shift of authority and responsibility. It is filled with a quiet confidence born from having accumulated the experience and understanding to function as the sole and ultimate decision-maker during flight. In the everyday world of life and living, the concept is the same.

Your "logbook entries" began the day you were born. And while it may feel like you're starting from scratch with this process of upgrading yourself to pilot in command, remember this: just as flight hours for pilots never expire, every single one of your experiences—the moments from your imaginative childhood, the times you applied and got rejected, the bruises from bumpy flights you've already taken—they *all* count and serve as experience. So, visit those corners of your mind and give yourself permission to attempt the wild, outlandish, high-risk, difficult journeys that, like mine, have far more reasons on paper to fail than to succeed. But elevate yourself above the prospect of failure and remember that in order to take these new journeys, you must create them. *You must think and act them into being*—just as I did with my around-the-world flight. Yes, it took mental clarity—but it also took tremendous amounts of preparation, focus, determination, and resources. And the journey would never have begun had I not quietly and continually upgraded myself to pilot in command.

As pilot in command, you've earned the privilege of living a life that is your own. Not everyone will understand your journey; humans are multi-dimensional, far more complex than the bullet points of our resumes, credit scores, and college degrees most people will remember us by. There is another group out there, however, who will be motivated by your standout mindset and your determination; this group is eager and thirsty to learn. And it is our logbooks of mistakes and achievements that will grant others permission to make mistakes of their own, as a natural part of the growth process.

But also remember that along with the intention to upgrade must also come the actual *execution*. This is where intention and action converge to become one bold, beautiful thing. So yes, the planning, the claiming, and the owning up to being pilot in command, the *thinking* it into being, all of that is essential. But there comes a moment when the doing stops and we are left with the elegant, open space of simply *being*. It is this *being* that gives us purpose and intention . . . but, as with everything, balance is involved.

You don't always have to assume the position of pilot in command

There are plenty of days when I know I am not acting with a pilot-in-command mindset; days when I'd rather leave the flying, the figuring out, and the navigating to someone else. And that, to me, is completely normal, completely acceptable. In fact, knowing when to shift from one mindset to another is not only courageous and commendable, but also an acquired and learned skill. The most skilled pilots, in my experience, maintain the lofty standards required of being a pilot in command in every aspect of their lives and in every role they fill.

We will not be the pilot in command of *every* situation we're in. That would be a terribly heavy burden to carry. However, we can function as a tailwind to others by staying true to the same level of professionalism, focus, and

40   attention as we would in their role while stepping back to let them take the lead. Relax a little, learn a lot, and you'll add more than you know by aiding in the creation of a calm cockpit.

Of course, there will be times we must relinquish our pilot-in-command status and yield it to someone else. For some of you, this probably causes an anxious reaction. I know it does for me. Because trust is involved when we relinquish this role, we've got to be clear about expectations for flight. Nerves can be calmed much more easily when openly discussing expectations around communication, direction, and emergencies; in fact, this is a much easier task to perform on the ground *before the plane ever takes flight* rather than waiting until you get up in the air or, even worse, during an emergency. That is what I mean about understanding as much as you can about all the flights you board in life. We can either function as pilot in command or as a passenger, depending on the circumstance. Both roles are vitally important, and appreciating the distinction between the two roles brings meaning and direction to life and living.

Always know when to assume control—even when it's uncomfortable

The universe's call to assume the position of pilot in command does not always arrive on our doorstep as a neatly wrapped invitation. Sometimes we must fight for the title; we must demand it. We must *will* it into being with our actions and our behavior, and often it's a split-second decision. You'll

be required to make difficult choices, and it will be up to you   41
to change course—often with little to no warning at all.

Just like the temperamental skies we choose to fly within, conditions change. Energy is transferred, and storms begin to form. Agreements shift. Our vision is obscured by conditions we didn't expect to fly through. In these moments, it can be easy to feel like our flight is spiraling out of control.

When you find yourself in these chaotic conditions, it is absolutely necessary to remind yourself that you are now pilot in command of your own flight. Even when you are not at the controls, you still choose which plane you board . . . until that door closes.

The example I'm about to share, while extremely uncomfortable, was pivotal in testing this theory, though I didn't realize it at the time.

It was 2007, obviously a vastly different world than the world we live in today. In the television and entertainment industry, the trajectory of reality shows was explosive. When I was approached by a group of experienced studio executives to talk about the possibility of my hosting a reality show that would involve a group of young women learning how to fly (what I initially thought might be an empowering, uplifting concept), I was eager to hear more. It combined everything I loved—airplanes, TV, travel—all with the added bonus of promoting women in aviation.

Serious discussions began. Concepts and details were developed. Agreements were even signed. Weeks later, I flew out to Burbank for what would be a full day of shooting promotional videos, ironing out the final details, and even sealing the deal. I imagine this material would have been used in a pilot episode. It was all very professional, very

42 *Hollywood.* Yes, I was wide-eyed, but I also felt I deserved to be there. I was training to become a pilot, and by the time the show would air, I'd have my license.

At the very end of that very long day, as production and high-level, closed-door meetings were winding down and it was time to get to the airport to fly home to Denver, the execs asked for one more quick meeting. This was a last-minute addition to the schedule. Carrying luggage and gear, I was asked to sit down in a cluster of chairs in the busy, bus-tling lobby of the hotel they had rented as production space.

What I thought was a quick, oh-and-one-more-thing en-counter in the lobby turned out to be far more than that. I still remember sitting there, slowing my breath to keep my composure as I listened to them casually toss in one more "small detail" they had decided about the show: they'd de-cided that the "winner" would be rewarded with a plane and would then embark on Amelia Earhart's around-the-world flight.

This turbulence felt as strong as a punch in the gut. Did I hear them correctly?

Here I was, in my early twenties, naively thinking all along that I'd be hosting a show about aviation, helping young women who were seriously interested in aviation to learn about the basics and beauty of flight, only to be told at the eleventh hour that the "winner"—with *no previous avi-ation experience allowed* in order to make the contest equal, I was told—would be attempting an around-the-world flight in Amelia's honor and memory.

It felt like not only an affront to me but an affront to the professionalism of the aviation industry, and while it is only my opinion, it felt like an affront to the memory of Amelia

Mary Earhart herself. The entire process felt flashy, skin-deep, way too glitzy, and flimsy.

In that single moment—as I was sitting in that lobby, feeling both exhilarated and exhausted from having spent the entire day on what had (up to that point, anyway) felt like a productive, meaningful day—the view became clear: I was just a passenger on their flight. I was not going to be the pilot in command at all but rather a clever and convenient coincidence. A passenger. A name.

Taking a deep breath, willing myself to stay professional, tears were pooling in my eyes. In hindsight, I realize that they made this decision *well* before that quick final meeting—which had turned out to not be a spontaneous add-on at all, but a carefully calculated decision presented by them as an "exciting opportunity."

They mistakenly assumed that I would be weak enough, impassive enough, and accepting enough (and in just enough of a hurry to make my flight) that I'd simply and quickly agree to it. They assumed I'd accept it all, hook, line, and sinker. They assumed that with the promise of big paychecks, travel, opportunity, and some level of "fame," it would be too much to turn down.

But they were wrong.

From a place I didn't even know existed within myself, as I was presented with an updated contract reflecting the changes they'd discussed, I used the word I'd rarely used before: No.

In that moment of "no," I was given clearance to fly toward many more moments of "yes" later in my own life. Trusting my gut when it just didn't *feel* right, I declared an in-flight emergency. I made a precautionary landing, knowing

44   my chances of survival were far higher now than having to eject or survive a forced landing with an unknown pilot at the controls.

When I shocked them all and said I could not go forward, I was told I'd wasted their time, money, attention, and energy.

Disappointed, yet oddly invigorated by the deep-down sense that things were unfolding exactly to plan, I communicated clearly, "If I would have known the full details of the plan before now, *nothing* would have been wasted, as I would never have agreed to join."

Spoken like a true pilot in command.

4

KNOW YOUR EMERGENCY PROCEDURES

THERE'S AN ADAGE IN AVIATION: A good pilot knows she'd rather be down here, wishing she was up there, than up there, wishing she was down here.

Like most adages, this one strikes a chord in its wit and truth, demonstrating the critical lesson that preparation and a thorough understanding of the aircraft procedure and the environments in which we fly are essential to reaching a pilot's goal of completing a safe flight, especially when an emergency occurs. While every flight comes with inherent risk, the pilot who has put in the hard work "down here" is equipped with more tools when things go wrong "up there."

46   From day one of training, pilots and flight crew are taught that rehearsing emergency procedure and rigorously preparing for worst-case scenarios, both physically and mentally, are what will allow them to operate from a position of confidence and calm if and when an emergency should occur—rather than from a position of panic, fear, and at worst, resignation. The world of aviation revolves around emergency preparedness. Just as we've all rehearsed how to survive the "unlikely event of a water landing" with flight attendants, the crew up front is also aware of the *specific* step-by-step rules to follow in the event of an emergency; these steps are designed to eliminate as many variables and decisions as possible in a way that facilitates maximum focus on the emergency at hand. This fixation on emergencies does not indicate doubt, fear, or weakness, but rather is a sign of preparation and prioritization. That's because once we know as much as we can about what could go *wrong,* we free ourselves to truly appreciate and enjoy all that's going *right!*

The biggest risk-takers I know are obsessed with preparing for emergencies, developing sound and sensible preemptive strategies for both survival on the side of the cliff as well as stepping off a cliff toward a new business venture. The principle is universal: demystifying what we fear can be accomplished by learning everything we possibly can about it, then creating a plan for when life's inevitable turbulence tests our skill.

By picking up the phone to schedule that long-overdue physical, for example, we are able to act from an informed perspective when it comes to our health. Through couples therapy or counseling, we can learn to effectively communicate with our partner. I urge you to reflect on how useful it would be to have a set of predetermined emergency procedures in your own life. Some examples are literal—for instance, learning how to stay aware of your surroundings in the case of an active shooter in your immediate vicinity—while at other times, your confidence will originate from deep within as you become the type of person who finds power in creatively optimizing upon what is still going right.

One successful electrical failure

Befriending emergency procedures does far more than just create a sense of calm amid cockpit chaos. They are actionable steps you must begin immediately to give you the best possible chance of survival. During an in-flight emergency, every second matters as gravity takes over. I speak from experience.

While working toward my commercial pilot's license at Denver's Centennial Airport, flying a rented Cessna 182, I was tested in a way I'll never forget. I'd just wrapped up a normal preflight exam, run-up of the engine, and had been cleared for takeoff. No more than three hundred feet above the runway, the entire cockpit went dark. No digital display. No fuel pump. No radio equipment. The list of what I no longer had access to was lengthy.

In this moment, I had been trained to focus on what I *did* have. An engine, a fellow pilot at my side, and a cell phone.

Before we communicate, we must first aviate and navigate. Checking circuit breakers, monitoring engine parameters, it was time to figure out how to land safely. Asking my capable copilot to my right to continue the climb-out,

48 I reached into my flight bag and grabbed my iPhone. Our radios were out, and I had to let the tower know we needed to land immediately. Fortunately, this close to the ground, the phone worked great. I spoke clearly over the airplane noise, stating, "Centennial Tower, this is November One Four Three Lima Whiskey. I'm the pilot in command, and we've experienced a full electrical failure on takeoff from Runway One Zero and would like permission to land as soon as possible."

The response was immediate, and it was clear: "November One Four Three Lima Whiskey, you are cleared to land on Runway Two Eight."

Assess the situation. React in ways that have been tested to work. Communicate your needs. Do your best to maintain a level head all the while.

Most emergencies take place in "critical phases" of flight—during ascent, descent, and changing weather conditions. As you face crisis and emergency in your own daily life, in the *personally* critical phases of flight, you must keep your own hands on your controls and be on the lookout for what could go wrong, but when it comes to focus, only zero in on what can go right rather than on what can go wrong. Fix the problem without *fixating* on it.

This focus is a form of *freedom*—a learned practice you can begin anytime, anyplace, in any emergency. I invite you to experience this freedom for yourself. Speaking from experience, I can promise you this: studying my homemade flashcards that covered emergency procedures prepared me so well for the worst, that when it counted most, I responded at my best.

Not all fears are created equal

This might surprise you, given that I've circumnavigated the globe, but flying over large bodies of water was my greatest fear. The thought of ditching our *Silver Lining,* the coveted Pilatus PC-12 NG, into the depths of the ocean felt even heavier because of the weight of the first Amelia's disappearance. These fears felt like they were unfolding in 3-D, combining the physical reality of surviving an ocean ditching, the responsibility of acting as pilot in command, and the self-imposed obligation I held to Amelia. I wanted to get it right on all accounts.

Before we get much deeper, let's have a quick preflight briefing: *80* percent of my around-the-world flight took place over open water. Let that sink in. Eighty-six of the 108 hours it took to circle the globe piloting a single-engine aircraft took place over the element that posed the biggest threat.

If I sound dramatic, that is intentional. Passing the point of no return around eighty nm offshore from Natal, Brazil, we were then too far out to turn back and make the runway to even attempt an emergency landing—but I knew what I signed up for, which meant mastering my *mental* game and putting myself in the right headspace was mandatory.

The word *headspace* really resonates, because the understanding I had not only of the aircraft as whole but especially of the Pratt & Whitney PT6 engine on which we relied freed up space to be logical about this highly unusual environment.

Here on the ground, we must create a rational plan for when the tides turn. For when the engine sputters. For when life takes a nosedive. When a relationship fractures. When

50 that pink slip arrives. When the doctor sits you down and gives you news that will shake you to your very core. These are the storms that life will bring . . . and being able to function at maximum capacity during these storms is what will allow us to deal with them efficiently and rationally. That means acting not as a robotic machine but rather a person, able to adapt and adjust to the environment we have chosen to fly within.

Of course, I'm describing times when we're at our best. There were plenty of hours during the around-the-world flight, especially in quiet stretches over lonely oceans, I struggled with my thoughts, my doubts, and my insecurities. Did I deserve to have an entire team of professionals helping me complete this goal? Was I wasting everyone's time to simply prove something to myself? Even during our greatest adventures, imposter syndrome can tag along for the journey.

When my headspace grew foggy, thoughts like this played on repeat: I'm not even related to Amelia. What if I'm also not a good enough pilot to safely complete this flight? I don't know if I could survive that kind of crash.

Paper tigers

We kicked off the second half of the world flight by departing from the idyllic paradise of Male International Airport in the Maldives, climbing to 27,000 feet above the vast expanse of the Indian Ocean. Toward the evening hours of this eight-hour mission, my doubts and fears began overtaking my thoughts, as the sounds of my critics—who I now think of

as my paper tigers, *my baseless fears and worries*—made their
presence known. I could almost see their jet-black stripes.

My inner dialogue went quiet, as if backed into a corner, fearful to fight back. *Who do you think you are? The real Amelia would be embarrassed to share her name with you! Who cares . . . if you were a real pilot, you'd be solo in a Lockheed Electra, like Amelia was. Anyone could fly around the world in a plane like this. You don't deserve to be up here.*

"Pilatus Five Eight November Golf," approach controllers called, snapping me back to the present moment. It was time to focus on the far more important task at hand: flying the plane. The thought that I'd dedicate any of my time in flight to the negative opinions of others, actual or imagined, is not something I like to admit. The world is quick to tell you to grow a thick skin when it comes to what others have to say. This outdated notion is one I reject wholeheartedly. I don't *want* a thick skin! Vulnerability is one of my core values, which means I need to stay open, soaking up all the emotion and meaning of this life.

Rather than fly amid contradicting voices, I countered fears with facts.

For instance, the thoughts creeping in telling me I didn't deserve to fly could be tempered by my inner logic, reminding myself that I was *already in flight*. My team of aviation experts from all over the world, who knew me well, had already made that decision, therefore it could not be decided in a meaningless tweet from a stranger having a bad day.

And at that moment, armed with the reality of all the work it had taken to get this far, I quieted the growl of the paper tigers by deciding for myself that I deserved to be there. By silencing the discouraging voices, we can learn

52   to hear what's actually being said, and in this case, it was a clearance to land at Singapore Changi Airport, where I'd be greeted by a team of our Honeywell experts along with school children who were excited to learn about flight.

I also knew that the final quarter of the flight would be grueling, so I needed to tap into every bit of logical focus I had inside. No longer could I give these paper tigers space in my mind; I'd enjoyed a quiet clarity in their absence and knew I was a far better pilot without them.

Unlatching the door of their cage (with a key I've since discovered I had in my pocket all along), I released my tigers—who had once held the power of flesh and bone—and I watched them tumble through the air, dissolving into the sea below.

That's just what paper tigers are: *they are paper.* Keep them locked up in your mind and their images can feel in-your-face ferocious. Negating their power with confidence and courage, we can render them ineffective and learn from our time spent in their presence. By facing them, we control them. We take away their power. Their stripes melt away.

Amelia Mary Earhart was known to have had an abject fear of flying over jungles; the thought of plummeting down into the dark, rich earth and being subsumed by the wild creatures—lions and tigers and other beasts of the jungle—was as frightening to her as being stranded in shark-infested waters is to me.

It's even been said that she put up wallpaper in her home that had a tiger design. Perhaps this was her attempt to face her fears and embrace her enemies by living in their midst? Perhaps this was her way of reminding herself that her fears were just that—paper tigers? They were not real.

They could be faced and even ripped down. This is precisely what we can do with our own fears: face them, rip them down, and eventually release them into the deepest depths of the ocean.

This is why her quote about facing fear and the importance of making swift, sound decisions still inspires me. "The most difficult thing is the decision to act. The rest is merely tenacity. The fears are paper tigers. You can do anything you decide to do. You can act to change and control your life and the procedure. The process is its own reward."

Today, I keep a print in my art studio of three tigers in a jungle, hiding among the leaves, eyeing my workspace, hungry and wild. These paper beasts serve to remind me they are always lurking in the shadows, ready to pounce. When they inevitably claw and crawl to get back into my mind, I'll take it as a sign to go all in . . . because nothing lures a paper tiger out into the open quite like the scent of a worthwhile idea.

Courage comes in waves

It's one thing to face your paper tigers—those empty, misguided fears can cling to your psyche like a drowning man clinging to a life raft, but they really only live in our minds. It takes work . . . but they *can* be destroyed.

It's another thing altogether to submerge yourself into the fear itself, learning to tread water alongside deeply personal fears that can *literally* drag you down underwater. This fear was *very* real as was the military-grade life raft I clung to in the very real, sloshing waves of the Atlantic Ocean.

54 Open water survival training

The open-water survival training exercise was (and remains) a mandatory insurance requirement for all flight crew members planning to cross bodies of water large enough that landing on the water is the only option in the event of an emergency.

Along with my all-male class of trainees, I awkwardly loaded onto the small training boat. Zipped up tight up from head to toe in our bright orange, plastic "Gumby" suits (to maintain our core body temperature in the icy waters), we were each pushed off the side of the boat, one by one. We had already been carefully trained in what to do once we hit the water. We knew that as we hit the cold, deep water, several things needed to happen: Above all, we needed to fight panic and immediately reorient ourselves in the water. Second, we had to visually locate—and then swim toward—our life rafts, which could be floating as far as fifty feet away. And once we reached them, we still needed to *deploy* them. I am not a strong swimmer; the instructors had to remind me to calm down, focus, and act. The shock of being submerged in such cold, deep water took my breath away.

I told myself, "Follow your checklist." I then located my life raft floating about thirty feet away—a bright yellow, two-by-two-foot square package, bobbing in the Atlantic. It took an incredible amount of effort to reach, and even once I reached it, I'd still need to deploy it. Teeth chattering furiously, I had been coached by experts on how to remain calm, even in the midst of this chaos. These ocean-based emergency drills placed me face-to-face with variables and elements in a somewhat controlled environment. By practicing out in the open water, my confidence grew, and in a very real way, I was better able to demystify the ocean itself.

Back in the simulation hangar, we faced even more fears in the Olympic-size swimming pool, where we participated in simulated rescues during disorienting lightning storms. There, we were loaded into the metal basket of a helicopter, hoisted to the ceiling above, then completely submerged in the pool. It was so realistic, there were several times I forgot we were training. This is precisely why the survival rate is so much higher for people who have been formally trained in these drills, who have rehearsed these maneuvers, and who have had the opportunity to develop the proper mental mindset that keeps you cool and calm during a water emergency.

But let's get back to the ocean. Fired by my own adrenaline now, I reached my life raft and yanked the red cord I had practiced pulling in the dry classroom, and I yanked it with every ounce of strength I had. It deployed immediately with a loud *swoosh* but unfortunately, it deployed facing *downward*—heavy, awkwardly-shaped, and because of its upside-down position, it also created a seal between the raft and water that I had to break.

Being underwater is what I feared most, but I knew I had to focus on what was possible. I took a deep breath and swam underneath the inflated raft. I can remember exactly what it sounded like under there, the sloshing water amplified and muffled all at once, and in that private moment I knew that this raft would only become an operational raft if I flipped it over.

With my body weight as leverage, I flipped the raft right-side up, and with what felt like the last ounce of energy

I had, I threw myself onto the raft's edge, allowing my limp body to take a moment's rest. In that moment, hanging off the side of that raft, I felt as safe and comfortable as I felt lying in the comfort of my own bed. Spent but renewed. Tired but ready and energized in a way I've never been energized before.

This is the thought I had while I lay bobbing in the water: *While all my girlfriends are off vacationing in Cabo, sipping margaritas poolside in their stylish bikinis, here I am, in my bright orange, plastic "Gumby" suit, hanging off the side of a lifeboat in the Atlantic Ocean.*

Not really knowing where all this new courage and openness to facing fears was coming from that day was okay by me. All I knew at that moment was that I was *exactly* where I was supposed to be.

Sharing skies, sharing seas

Each of us was left on our own, bobbing life raft for about thirty minutes before the rescue team came to pick us up. I am sure that even those moments—those empty, disorienting spans of time adrift in the open sea waiting for the rescue boat to arrive—were deliberately built into the exercise. We needed time to process everything that had just transpired, time to imagine what it would be like to truly wait to be rescued. Being able to sit in the midst of that moment—out on the open water rather than in a cramped classroom or a simulation booth—was a vital part of the learning experience.

The boat returned and loaded up our group of exhausted, but now more experienced, trainees. One of the young men who helped me aboard the boat leaned toward me and pointed toward the distant shore. He looked at me for a moment.

"See that chapel way over there?" he asked, pointing. "That's where Amelia Earhart and George Putnam were married," he told me. "She was a woman pilot so I thought you might think that's neat."

I certainly did.

Responding with a salty, squinted smile, I had that familiar, comforting feeling of "Of *course* she's here . . ."

Why wouldn't she be? I'd just completed survival training in the Atlantic Ocean she successfully crossed solo sixty-seven years prior. Proving again what she represents for women in aviation today: Freedom. Fearlessness. Determination.

All of it, wrapped up into one.

5

EMBRACE THE SOLO FLIGHT

IN THIS FLIGHT LESSON, we're venturing into uncontrolled airspace, navigating away from the traditional definition of "solo flight," to reveal yet another way to pilot life's journey. Early in my flight training, I associated "solo flight" with being the kind of pilot that never needed *anyone else around*. In my head, I picture her proud and confident . . . but maybe a little lonely, even scared.

Today, I choose a different way to fly solo; a singular, personal decision of risk versus reward that allows me to learn to trust myself in those quiet moments, alone at my own controls. This is experiential knowledge, then, and I offer it to you here in hopes that it will illuminate your own flight path.

All too often, life decides when it's time for us to fly solo: The severing of a relationship. The death of a spouse. The loss of a job. Even something as seemingly innocuous (but also potentially devastating) as the moment a single parent must say goodbye as their child flies away from the nest. Forced solo flights are even a reality of the coronavirus pandemic that we happen to be living through as I write this book, from quarantine and isolation to the tragic loss of human life. In times of loss, we will be called to make and trust our intuitive decisions to best keep us in flight. These solo flights are where character is built and tested but can often feel clunky and forced because of their random nature. *Do your best, even if your landing is a little rough.*

Here, I want us to peel back and reveal that deeper, more expansive definition of "solo" that includes, for instance, the kind of solo flight that *feels like* you're alone, even though you're surrounded by others. Even with another human literally inches away, vulnerability, isolation, and pain feel like the only companions for miles.

Take heart in what I'm about to say next: solo flights only need to remain solo until *we invite* the perspective, insight, and assistance of others into the cockpit with us. All of us have more copilots than we realize; they're waiting in the wings, eager to offer support, guidance, or their simple, silent presence. Think of a time when you've been asked to step in and "fly the plane" for a friend who needed a moment to regain composure. When we lend the extra couch and a set of sheets to a friend without passing judgment or show with our actions that we will be there when we're needed, even if it's just to simply listen, even in the middle of the night.

This leads me to an incredibly powerful principle: many of the *solo journeys* we're struggling our way through (even now are *solo* because no one else knows we've taken flight). For example, when I allow myself to spiral into all the "what-ifs" about family health, finances, and all the other worries swirling in my own head, I'm on a solo flight and ignoring what really matters: flying the plane in the present moment. One quick phone call for clarification, a little research, being the first to say I'm sorry. These are all instant ways to turn down the pressure on solo flights stress, granting yourself permission to expand your mental, physical, and emotional space around you in a way that allows you to experience your flight on a far more meaningful level.

As a young pilot completely new to the world of aviation, I often felt isolated and alone. I felt like I didn't *belong*. It wasn't only because I still felt like I was carrying the burden of trying to prove myself as Amelia Rose Earhart but because there were (and still are) so few women in aviation. (Recent FAA statistics confirm that in 2019, only 7.9 percent of the nation's pilots were female.)

That there are so few of us in the industry definitely made me feel like I was flying a solo flight. But I will also admit that I wasn't asking anyone to fly *with* me, figuratively or literally. Fearful of reaching out to other more experienced female pilots for advice, guidance, or mentorship, I developed a self-reliant outer shell that only intensified these feelings of isolation. My insistence on flying solo required me to work harder and longer, and it became a pretty lonely way to travel, but as we've discussed, we are not locked on train tracks. We can change our course and modify our behavior any time we choose.

Over time, as my confidence grew, and as I began connecting with other women in aviation, I was able to experience the joy that comes from accompanying someone else on her solo flight. I began to reach out, to find mentors, and eventually, to mentor young women interested in aviation. But it was those lonely, vulnerable, initial moments of my career that led me to these bolder, braver places where I stand today. And today I also recognize the power of mentorship and comfortable camaraderie because I once yearned for it so deeply myself. And now I witness it in action through the Fly with Amelia Foundation with each scholarship awarded to a young woman already demonstrating these principles simply through applying.

The lesson here is that we often hold the power to decide whether we want to fly solo or not. And when we don't, it doesn't always mean that we're weak or frightened or not up to the task; it can simply mean we've decided to make our journey even more *our own* by expanding the perspectives we're willing to consider. The decision is ours to make.

The airplane doesn't care who's flying it

The European Business Aviation Convention & Exhibition (EBACE), held in Geneva, Switzerland, is regarded as one the most important aviation conferences in the world. My presence was important in 2014 because I'd be attempting my flight around the world in a matter of months. Pilatus Aircraft (which also happened to be based in Switzerland) had a large presence at the conference. I had flown in commercially for a week of press interviews about my upcoming trip and to generate support for and enthusiasm about the journey itself. In addition, many of the other companies that were sponsoring my flight were in attendance as were all of the biggest names and the heaviest hitters in aviation. The stakes were high, and so was the visibility.

I remember it like it was yesterday, looking out onto the vast airfield, the snow-covered Swiss Alps as our dramatic backdrop, while in the foreground stood some of the finest, most highly sophisticated aircraft in the world. And there in the center of them all, stood a Pilatus PC-12 NG, confidently gleaming in the sun.

Each day of the conference was booked with press events, panel discussions, and appearances, and this was the first one. I was told to meet some reporters and photographers, along with sponsor representatives, at the steps of the plane. It would be a quick meeting before the day's events started. Someone suggested I stand on the steps of the plane, looking back over my left shoulder toward the camera. Anyone could see it would make for a great shot: "Amelia Earhart, snow-covered Swiss Alps at her back, standing on the stairs of the Pilatus PC-12 NG, preparing to fly around the world."

Since this was a business conference, not an airshow, I was wearing professional dress and heels as I stood and posed for photos. Up there on those steps, I was enjoying a moment of proud solo flight, letting it sink in, right there with my whole team present. Each expert in front of me was spending part of the day making sure I was supported. What a monumental task it was to even make it this far!

My moment of reflection was interrupted by a man's

voice from the back of the small crowd. His perfectly pressed pilot's uniform, adorned with four gold bar epaulets, matched an amused expression I recognized as a challenge.

"How would you like a pilot in that photo with you?" he asked. "If you want, I can show you some of the bells and whistles on this plane."

This time, it was my turn to wear the amused expression.

In that moment—with cameras whirring, with all my sponsors waiting to see how I'd react, and with members of the aviation media present—all eyes were on me to fly *this* particular solo flight with *this* particular pilot with dignity, strength, grace, and decorum. If I had turned to my team and sulked over hurt feelings or tried to embarrass him, how could my team expect me to represent the goals of women in aviation when they weren't around?

Reminding myself that the airplane does not care whether it's being flown by a man or a woman, it only knows when it's being flown correctly, I stood tall in my own truth, in my own heels.

"There *is* a pilot in my photo," I answered directly.

Pushing just a little further, he leaned over, and he looked inside the plane to look for the pilot. Someone from my team politely let him know I was, in fact, the pilot who would be flying the same model of the Pilatus aircraft around the world in a matter of a few short months.

He walked away, brushing off the whole interaction. Once he was gone, something miraculous happened in our small crowd. Everyone nodded their own little unique acknowledgement for how I'd stood my ground in that solo-flight moment. The next morning, 12,000 event attendees woke to a trade show magazine cover with a headline reading "Women's Dreams Fly with Amelia."

64 This is your flight, Amelia

On June 26, 2014, sitting at the end of the runway before takeoff from Oakland, I looked over at my copilot Shane Jordan and said, "We're about to fly around the world."

In that moment, I wanted to honor his commitment to being a part of this team, and he knew that. Then Shane gave me a gift I didn't even know I needed. "This is *your* flight, Amelia."

Never had I felt so seen in the cockpit, and for me, Shane's wholehearted response set the bar for what it means to be a man who truly supports women in aviation.

Nearing Lae, Papua New Guinea, we were mentally and physically exhausted. This was also the last place Amelia Mary had been seen before her disappearance. The airport looked deserted when we landed, until several large, heavily armed men in utility trucks drove straight onto the runway, pulling up directly to the left side of the plane where I sat at the cockpit. They stared up silently at me. Tension and anxiety were high.

My hand shook as I opened the door to present arrival paperwork. The men glared back angrily, repeating the word *pilot*. Pointing to myself didn't work either. They were waiting for *Shane* to speak, as the man on the flight. He saw the fear building up in me, the exhaustion, the feeling of being almost overwhelmed, but instead of taking over, he looked me in the eye and reminded me with the same respect he did on the runway in Oakland, "This is your flight, Amelia."

From touchdown that afternoon to our sunrise departure the following morning, our experience in Papua New Guinea was met with complicated and nuanced situations requiring a balance between authority, compromise, and respect in all directions, and Shane was at my side each time, reminding me that this was my flight but that he was there just in case things went wrong.

I used to naively think that for my around-the-world flight to matter to anyone, I'd need to go it alone. Today, I see how much pressure I placed on myself, and I see how far I've come.

While solo flights are an incredible feat, there's a special form of bravery reserved for those unafraid to ask for a little help along the way.

6

ACT UPON GROUND EFFECT

CONSIDER THIS AVIATION CONCEPT: seconds after a plane takes off, while within one wingspan of the ground, circular airflow around the wing gives a helpful, buoyant push. Here we are in *ground effect*, benefiting from the cushion of air between earth and wing. For the plane, it's an advantageous aerodynamic phenomenon. For me, this time and space has always felt a little bit magical, as if the atmosphere wants me to optimize on this moment.

This is not a common analogy. I've assigned personal meaning to this fleeting transition of extraordinary energy, potential, and transformation that lies within these brief moments because the trajectory of my own life has been deeply influenced by both the practice and principles of seizing the potential of ground effect, in both a literal and a figurative sense.

In this Flight Lesson, I want to invite you to experience and explore the magnificent potential that exists within this powerful pocket of buoyancy. I want you to actually *experience* this sensation of floating, of hovering between the choice of two options, and to recognize that when you are in ground effect, you—and you alone—have the power to either propel yourself upward into full flight or yield to gravity and allow yourself to quickly sink back down to earth. So much of our emotional, mental, and spiritual growth depends on what we decide to do within this small, sacred space, making this small, sacred space an incredibly special place to be.

These pockets of potential and possibility are waiting for you in your own life, too. They're constantly bubbling up and unfolding around us, but our rational adult minds are trained to tamp them down and extinguish them before they can even ignite into a spark. "Why bother? Someone else is probably out there doing it better than we ever could," we tell ourselves.

What do you do when the first, gentle wisp of a new idea floats into your mind? What do you *do* with it? Do you give it the space, the energy, and the attention it deserves, or do you simply drop your daydream back down on the runway before it even has a chance to gain momentum, exit ground effect, and take flight? The unlimited potential of the mind unleashes only when we listen to these pure, powerful moments and let them linger. Can't stop thinking about that idea? Then push forward without fear. Look around. The world is filled with concepts that come to life—wild, outlandish ideas just like yours—because their creators chose to optimize on ground effect. They took that early cushion of lift, excitement, and momentum and transitioned into full flight. You can do this, too.

It's equally important to understand that in this moment of "floating," in this precious, powerful moment of *becoming*, a tremendous amount of energy is being generated, transferred, and exchanged. Think about it: for a plane that weighs *thousands of pounds* to move from an earthbound to an airborne state requires extraordinary and precise amounts of momentum and force. The same energy, momentum, and force—on a different scale, of course—are required to bring an idea aloft. And just as the pilot in command is the only one who can exert this energy, *you* are the only one who can generate enough energy, force, and momentum to propel your dreams, your hopes, and your latest ideas into being. Both the decision and the act belong to you.

These moments of choice and these energy-filled sparks live within *all* of us the instant we commit, and they die when they're dismissed. The fact that they are so fleeting makes them even more precious. Why? It reminds us to be watchful for these moments and gentle enough with ourselves so that when they arrive, we must allow ourselves the luxury of exploring them. You do not need to be afraid. This is not the time for overthinking.

When that first, faint pull of a new idea or an exciting new interest floats into our consciousness, most of us shove it away as an annoyance or a distraction. As children, we were one with our imagination, but our adult brains tend to filter out what is less than logical. You can stay stuck in ground effect while you decide, but letting negative "inner speak"—*Will I look silly? What if this doesn't work? What will my colleagues say? Who told me I could pursue this idea without having a sound, rational reason?*—has a way of drowning out the childlike curiosity we were born with, causing our once-invigorating ideas to land with a thud.

Author, psychiatrist, and Holocaust survivor Viktor Frankl once wrote that "between stimulus and response, there is a space. In that space is our power to choose our response." And in our response, "lies our growth and freedom."

Just as the airplane transitions from ground to air, a contemplative moment spent with an idea that's yours and yours alone is an investment in your higher self.

Love at first flight

My parents' decision to name me Amelia Earhart did not guarantee I'd be born with a natural, driving desire to fly. As a young girl and a teenager, I'd always been *interested* in flight, but I'd often amp up my personal excitement to satisfy the eager Amelia Earhart enthusiasm surrounding the topic. No one in my family flew airplanes, so it was up to me to explore if I'd even enjoy it. In June 2004, I had saved up enough for my first lesson, a discovery flight in Boulder, Colorado, and thank goodness I did, because that was the day the small spark of interest for flight ignited into a roaring flame.

Imagine as a child, growing up with constant inquiries from "grown-ups" and peers asking, "So, will you ever be a pilot?" and "When will you, Amelia Earhart, learn to fly?"

70 and the resulting disappointment on their faces when I had to tell them the truth: I wasn't sure! Late in my teens, I even got tired of hearing my own responses; I felt I was apologizing for something that, in my mind, was a major life decision. It was time to just try it out. I'd been toying with this idea of becoming a pilot all my life; it was time to get out of ground effect to see if I'd sink or soar.

I was a student at the University of Colorado-Boulder and, like most college students, had little extra money to throw around for any extracurricular activities—much less for flight lessons, which are not inexpensive. My college years were as busy as the years I planned the world flight, working three or four part-time jobs to offset the significant cost of flight lessons. The cycle of saving for months then spending it all on a few quick lessons meant I spent about eight years working toward my private license.

That discovery flight, as routine and rudimentary as it may have been for the instructor, felt like the beginning of a deeply important relationship with me. The cloudless, brilliant blue sky presented a stark and welcoming contrast to the gruff, no-nonsense flight instructor who was not at all amused by this young college student named Amelia Earhart showing up on his airfield saying she wanted to learn how to fly.

What happened next tells the story of love at first flight: Climbing into the Cessna, I began scanning the cramped cockpit. The leather seats were cracked from years sitting out in the sun, and when I opened the door, I was hit with the smell of fuel rags and sweat and the light groan and creak of the small Cessna 172 as it accepted our weight. One of the gauges even read INOP, meaning that while the plane itself was airworthy, this particular knob was "inoperative." This plane felt more like a tractor than a flying machine.

As we rolled, bumped, and squeaked down the runway, quickly picking up speed, I felt it for the first time: that *moment*. We were technically off the ground, but it didn't quite feel like flying; I held my breath while we floated in this open space. That roiling energy as the plane struggled to break the bonds of earth. The instructor even said it, "We're in ground effect now. If we pull back on the yoke, the nose will lift and we will climb, but if we release some of the back-pressure, the nose will come back down . . ." And suddenly, I was in the midst of this rumbling, transformative energy.

We pulled back on the yoke, his force exerting the exact amount of pressure to peel us away from the earth as I gently followed his control inputs on the dual controls. We had made the choice to separate from the runway, giving into the power of that beautiful, buoyant moment. If that plane could talk, I imagined it was whispering to me, "I want to fly."

I whispered back, "I want to fly, too."

In that brief, potential-filled moment, in that split second of being in ground effect—between preparing to be airborne and *being* airborne—I'd found the place where I'd come to cultivate my most meaningful ideas. In that space, all judgement, all doubt, all the expectations and inquiries from others, were suspended. I memorized the unique feeling of pushing through ground effect, knowing I'd need to re-create this powerful sensation: I was in flight and everything else fell away.

We spent less than an hour in flight, yet a part of me had been transformed. Being named after a pilot and truly taking flight were two different things entirely. While I had no control over my name, I had found new confidence in a sliver of airspace.

72   Be patient in ground effect

A complicated quality of sacred spaces (like ground effect) lies in their brief and fleeting nature. But these sacred spaces are everywhere, constantly unfolding around us, hiding in the ordinary moments of the day to day, asking for our attention. We must give ourselves permission to purposefully place ourselves in the right mindset; a mindset will allow us to seek, befriend, and explore what could be . . . and when the time is right, to *pursue*.

Sadly, most of the great ideas we have, most of the untraceable visions that bubble up to the surface of our consciousness, are never even allowed to breathe the breath of life. They never really get out of ground effect; they never fully soar. I am not saying all ideas are worth diving into but be careful not to become the kind of person who automatically sends new ideas straight back to the ground without consideration.

At any given moment, I've got all sorts of ideas floating at various altitudes in my mind, and I am constantly revisiting and refueling them as needed. Just as I spent eight years in pursuit of my pilot's license, I hope you take pride in the determination and resilience it takes to accomplish pursuits to which you dedicate significant amounts of time. Hovering over possibility can be *helpful* in granting the time and the space needed to plan, to strategize, to save up, and, if necessary, to train and prepare but there will come the moment when it's time to trust yourself to pull back on the controls and take flight. It is an acquired skill, and one I never plan to let fade.

Being a student, working, launching a successful career as a television journalist, relocating—combined with all the surprises, setbacks, sorrows, and joys that come with living life—I know now that I completed my goal of becoming a pilot at exactly the right moment; and while life may have dictated my pace, I wasn't about to let it dictate or limit my direction.

I believe cultivating and maintaining a childlike curiosity about the world around me is what keeps my mind's door open to the outlandish, unusual, and unlikely concepts I enjoy most. The fire of my own curiosity and enthusiasm is at the heart of my most creative and meaningful attempts, whispering and tugging at me to just *try it*. Next time something excites you, succumb to the honest, raw enthusiasm of befriending your inner child and just see where it takes you.

None of this is easy. None of this is automatic or reflexive or a guaranteed success. As I've already mentioned, exiting ground effect is a *learned skill*; it's a skill that is acquired over time, with hard work and perseverance. But as you plot your course and as you evaluate all the options, ideas, hazards, and open spaces around you, do your best to resist the gravitational pull of your adult mindset that whispers, "You don't have time. Stop being silly. That's not who you *are*."

Whether your idea is loud and bold for the world to see, or just a quiet, private, inner stirring, pushing it toward becoming a reality will never be as simple as "just doing it." For example, for two years my around-the-world flight was littered with complex challenges as I tested the idea in ground effect, but never once did I let it slip through my fingers and fall back down to earth. My childlike enthusiasm combined with my understanding of the potential the idea held created a mixture that *others* began to want to see take flight.

Did I have doubts and anxieties? Of course. But even in moments when I felt discouraged and doubtful about the flight, I never let that sacred space slam shut. The crack in the door that let the light in was the knowledge that the decision to move this from a vague abstraction to a rock-hard reality belonged only to *me*—and today I am incredibly proud that I was able to keep the idea aloft. I fed that fire. I stoked that flame. I refused to let the doubts and fears from myself, or others extinguish it. You can, too.

In this life, understand the aspirations we feel at the center of ourselves, the hopes and dreams that must be intentionally cultivated and consciously nudged into fruition, are sometimes the most precious of all. The worry, care, thought, and focus we invest in these lifelong accomplishments define our character. To the mother who just finished putting her two children through college yet always dreamed of the day when she might be able to go to grad school herself: enroll in that class. To the entrepreneur who spent years holding on to the distant idea of launching her own business: apply for that loan. Be intentional and start your engine. One definitive, physical action can often set off an entire chain of events, just like my first flight lesson did.

Life is meant to be lived. To be explored. To be conquered and fully embraced, with courage and confidence. Its branches are meant to be shaken rigorously with every ounce of energy you possess so that *every* piece of fruit can fall from the tree.

This is why I've been able to make space in my life for a new passion—art—in a "no-rules" way that brings balance, peace, and a playful spirit to my days. I have placed enough trust in myself to push forward with this passion, and each time I pick up my paintbrush, I get to know myself and the world more intimately. You, too, can give yourself permission to leave the ground and explore new directions.

As a final benefit, I also want to share that ground effect is where I let my mind go to play, entertaining unconventional solutions and contemplating outlandish observations about any and everything. I grow a lot here, getting to know myself and what I am capable of creating, and I hope you can, too. Between stimulus and response, between being and becoming, *this* is the sacred space where imagination becomes reality and concepts become concrete. While we cannot locate this spot on a map, or point to its precise definition in a dictionary, I'm certain it is central to all our greatest journeys.

7

ENGAGE WITH YOUR FLIGHT CREW

LET'S CLEAR OURSELVES to venture into uncontrolled airspace again, just as we have in earlier Flight Lessons. Let's peel back the layers to reveal a more expansive way of thinking about the many "flight crews" we contribute to in our lives. From this more elevated perspective, we give ourselves clearance to explore fresh new ways of thinking, new ways of *being*.

Here, we will come to understand and appreciate with renewed intensity the vital role that a flight crew—a cohesive, purpose-driven unit made of many but functioning as one—can play by helping us fly higher, faster, and more efficiently than we would solo.

But first, we must understand that the best flight crew is
not composed of crew members who simply perform their
individual jobs without error. While this is obviously critical
to each flight's success, there's far more involved than individual proficiency. The best flight crews are composed of
crew members who are aware enough, responsible enough,
and trusting enough to fly *in the present moment*, setting ego
aside for the success of a mission.

It may sound idyllic, but I speak from experience: through
collective responsibility and accountability between all members, an average, ordinary flight crew can transition into an
extraordinary, high-functioning unit by simply making small,
intentional changes. Put simply, while we do not all need to
be certified pilots, engine mechanics, baggage handlers, and
flight attendants, we *do* all need to be on the same mission.
This kind of emotional, situational, and mental dexterity requires heightened awareness and an all-in attitude from everyone involved. This applies not just in a flight crew but
within any kind of team or collaborative unit of which you
find yourself a part. This is not a casual take on teamwork. If
it sounds like a lot of work and attention, that's because it is.

Requiring this level of cohesion will inherently shrink the
pool of potential flight crew members with whom you'll
align. That is why these types of teams are so special and
so rare. Until you've experienced this type of collaborative,
unimpeded flow firsthand, it's tough to believe it can even
be achieved. But I assure you it can. Therefore, find the best
possible flight crew you can locate and *engage* that crew so
that they all work together, as one.

Going forward, let us commit to a fresh, new definition
of teamwork. It's one which also requires us to think from
multiple perspectives. Let's dig a little deeper.

78   Among the best flight crews there exists an inherent equality. No, this doesn't mean that responsibilities and duties are casually *interchangeable*—a functional hierarchy is what keeps airplanes in flight—but it does mean that each member must cultivate a shared sense of belonging and accountability. In aviation, there are built-in methods to ensure any crew member can speak up freely when something feels amiss or off-balance without fear of retribution or rebuke. For instance, some critical checklists are performed by multiple crew members to ensure two minds have the chance to agree about critical decisions. Each flight crew member has the duty to address safety concerns directly—not as a personal affront or a stinging criticism against a crew member of a higher rank but as proof that the ultimate mission and success of the flight belongs to every crew member on board.

The same should hold true in our lives at home and at work: ask questions when the time is right, understand how those around you spend their time, and communicate your shared goals clearly and openly. These important conversations heighten your environmental, situational, and often-neglected *emotional* awareness. When you've cultivated the right crew, all members will naturally act as one for the common good . . . and you'll know it when you feel it.

Yes, our skies will still have random storms to navigate, but I promise, with these higher standards come lengthy stretches of flight where the air is as smooth as glass.

Obviously, whether you're a member of a flight crew or a staffer on a sales team, those with whom we partner are going to occasionally come up short. We cannot show up at our absolute best every single day, and this model accounts for that. When something feels off-balance, the best teams have those tough but necessary conversations. Strong team members address issues respectfully but directly, leading with sincerity. "I'm sensing you've got a lot on your mind today. I'm here to listen and adjust. Let us make a plan here on the ground rather than waiting until after this project has taken flight."

To be this intuitive about and aware of our flight crew's state, we've got to listen and listen well. This deliberate shift and purposeful expansion in our thinking gives everyone on the team full clearance to ask, "Are you sure about that, Captain? Let's run the fuel pump test one more time. These numbers look off to me," before costly mistakes are made. When we break down the walls of who is "supposed to" speak up when something just feels imbalanced or off-course, we exponentially expand the awareness of our entire crew, which is good for everyone involved. And once we genuinely believe our voices are valued—and that our voice is a vital part of the collective team—will we speak up with 100 percent honesty.

At this level, a team operates as the sum of all its parts, no longer as individuals engaged in their own, singular pursuits. Put simply, tests and exams are what keep us proficient in *how* we fly, but it's up to us, as a cohesive flight crew, to hold one another up to our agreed-upon *why*.

"Are you sure about that, captain?"

That aviation is in many ways militaristic in its precision—the constant checklists, the painstakingly detailed preparation, the confirmation of confirmations—is the very reason that aviation is so safe. Although this may sound counterintuitive, the closer a flight crew or a team is able to operate within the confines of the agreed-upon rules and regulations, the more freedom they will eventually be able to enjoy as the flight (or the project) progresses. For once we have proven we can observe and adhere to rules, then and only then are we trusted to enter the wide-open airspace of all that the sky holds, where we have the freedom to simply *fly*. In aviation, the less experience we have, the closer we must stay to home base. In life, the same principle applies: we gain trust in our field, and from our colleagues and superiors, by demonstrating that we respect the established framework rather than breaking the rules like a disobedient teenager.

But I want to get back to this notion of collective accountability for a moment, to return to the importance of feeling comfortable and confident enough to ask your crew member—no matter who it may be—"Are you sure about that? Do you want to check once more . . . *just to be sure?*" It is these checks and balances that catch critical errors and keep crews in the air.

As I look back at my own early life, I realize now, with the clarity of sixteen years of experience (and hindsight that until only recently felt like an embarrassing stab of regret), how much heartache I could have avoided if I'd asked *myself*, "Are you sure about that, Amelia?" when I was trying to figure out my relation to Amelia Mary Earhart.

In my early twenties, I was conflicted and more than a little anxious about finding a conclusive answer to the question lurking around seemingly every corner: "So, how exactly are you related to the first Amelia Earhart?" Mom and Dad would offer the vague reminder, "We've always been told that we're somehow related to her . . . ," but this was only a partial answer that did little to calm the unease I felt living with the full name.

When I'd finally earned enough money to hire a genealogist who confirmed that there was, indeed, "a distant relationship" but who stopped short of a definitive, conclusive
answer until she could conduct additional research (which,
of course, required several thousand more dollars that
I simply did not have), I felt almost relieved to settle for her
half-answer. This middle ground was as comfortable a setting
as I could manage in this decidedly uncomfortable situation.

Although I couldn't see it with clarity then, I certainly
can now. It was more than not having the money for additional research; I was too frightened to face the final, complex answer. I'd just barely begun feeling confident living
with the name; if it turned out I wasn't related, would
I need to start over and reject all emotional and psycholog-
ical connections to her? It was daunting and overwhelming,
and, at that age, I simply didn't understand how important the knowledge—the confidence of *knowing*—would
turn out to be later in my life. For a long time, the middle
ground was much more comfortable. I didn't understand,
then, how much time and energy I was wasting wondering
and worrying about whether I was related or not; precious
time and energy I could have poured into positive, productive pursuits. Like flying. Like school. Like living my life in
a way that was authentic and fearless. I was holding on to
the name because I was desperately afraid it would be taken
away from me with a definitive (and possibly negative)
answer. I was afraid.

In my young, naive view, holding on to any connection
was better than none. Today, I can say with certainty that
if I could go back and copilot my younger self through
that process, I would have gently reminded that audacious
dreamer, "Amelia, I know you're trying your hardest to align

yourself with the incredible pilot you're named after, but this is your sky to fly just as much as it was hers. Look deeper. Whatever we find out, we'll be just fine."

I would tell her to hire a second researcher and not stop until the full picture was in view. While I cannot go back in time and fix my mistake, I can forgive my younger self for letting fear hold me back.

Today, I realize that we must face the tough questions in our lives with courageous intention, no matter the outcome. If the result is out of our control, which most certainly was for me, we need only concern ourselves with how we respond to the outcome. We must cultivate within ourselves a driving desire to seek answers, even if those answers hurt when they do arrive. It was this fear—the preposterous idea that if I wasn't related to her, I'd be less valuable to the world—that eventually caused me even greater pain and embarrassment.

Today, I operate with a pilot's mindset, not just when I am flying but when my feet are on solid ground as well. Like the pilot that I am, my actions and behaviors spring from a desire for *accuracy*, for accountability, for clarity, and for solid, evidence-based understanding. For me, it is the only way to fly. I didn't know that then. I know it now.

The reason I can look back and forgive my twenty-something-year-old self for not researching my connection to Amelia as fully as I should have is because I *can*. I *can* forgive myself and accept my missteps, because my missteps are an important part of my journey and my trajectory, too. They have led me to precisely where I am today, strong in identity, confidence, and self-acceptance, where I can both laugh at and love myself despite the parts of my story that feel embarrassing to explain. We all have the capacity to learn from our past missteps and forgive ourselves for our past mistakes; it is just difficult to access. Today I know that I am enough. I have mentored other young women new to aviation. I have circumnavigated the globe. I have grown, evolved, and become stronger and wiser as a result of my past experiences (both positive and negative), I am enjoying the ongoing process of becoming the very best version of myself that I can possibly be.

The lesson here is this: we must always be *eager* to pursue the truth, even if it hurts. Even if it's scary. Today I do not waste time on possibilities unless I'm serious about pursuing them. I am not afraid to embrace and pursue the truth, because the truth is where freedom lives. This is where I want to live. Always remember that once you embrace all that you are—all your foibles, flaws, strengths, insecurities, vulnerabilities, *all of it*—you no longer have to live in fear. You no longer have to languish in limbo. Face the questions that stand before you full on. Face them, and *answer* them, even when it's painful. It has been the passage of time, the accumulation of wisdom and experience, and the eye-opening journey of my flight around the world that has led me to a place where I stand in clarity and peace.

Today, I know who I am, and I am enjoying the journey of continued self-discovery. I am not related to Amelia, but I certainly have a clear and healthy understanding of how I relate to her. This much I know with certainty: she has been and will continue to be a driving force in my life and a tremendously positive influence.

Today, when I'm asked if I'm related to Amelia Earhart, I can confidently answer, "Nope . . . but I was named after her," with a smile that comes from appreciating all the hard work it took to arrive at such a simple answer.

84 Clarity through communication

Aviation, as I have mentioned before, is all about communication. Long before the plane even leaves the ground, clear and open communication between all crew members is not only expected, but also *required*. This is why the preflight briefing is a vital and mandatory part of every flight. Here is where the entire crew—pilot, copilot, flight attendants, ground crew, anyone who has a role to play in the safe and successful completion of the flight—comes together to review, discuss, and agree upon the details of the flight. That the preflight briefing is *spoken aloud* in a succinct and orderly fashion with all crew members listening intently, engaging, questioning, and clarifying, *sets the tone for the entire flight.*

Wouldn't it be wonderful if we were able to communicate with such precision and intention in our daily lives? To be able to stand amid our team members, colleagues, or family members with a collective, clear-eyed vision of the mission we are trying to accomplish and communicate as one, single entity?

This is not a pipe dream. It is a realistic, attainable goal. In your own life, remember that it is the teams, the flight crews, and the functional groups that are most closely unified in their mission—and most capable of communicating that mission aloud in clear, concise terms—that will achieve ultimate and enduring success. Whether it is a family member experiencing a crisis or an office manager grappling with a disengaged employee, it will be *communication* among the entire team, the entire flight crew, that elevates them above their own turbulence and steers them toward a clear, unobstructed flight path. This takes mental work as well. To get to this open airspace requires the right *headspace*. Mindset matters.

Think of the manager who grows increasingly frustrated with the underperforming employee yet does nothing to attempt to communicate with that employee in a way that will bring about positive change. When this happens, resentments build on both sides. Anger, fear, and feelings of futility begin to fester. These negative byproducts will create drag on *any* flight. They push us off course, away from our intended destination. This doesn't have to happen.

In situations where precision, situational awareness, and concise communication are mandatory and fully expected, adopting a pilot-like mentality toward communication can be incredibly effective. When team members can regularly turn to one another as part of a pre-established, preflight briefing (weekly or daily, perhaps?) to engage in this kind of precise and powerful communication, the team's chances for ultimate success increase exponentially. Especially when there is doubt or discord, give yourself permission to ask, "Are we on the same page? Are our goals perfectly aligned? Are we acting as a single, unified entity? And if not, what must we do to get ourselves back on track?" This is what will elevate your journey. And this is what will give us confidence, a clearer sense of direction, and an abiding sense of collective belonging.

86 Cultivating Trust

If this kind of consistent, brutally honest communication is to be woven into the fabric of any growing company or integrated into the structure of any struggling family or applied as both a principle and a practice by *any* team seeking growth, healing, betterment, or new direction, then it must be practiced at all levels . . . by everyone.

The entry-level employee should have license and permission to respectfully question his or her superior or ask for clarification without fear of backlash or retribution—not to prove the superior wrong or to question the person's competence or authority but to establish and maintain a clear understanding of the collective mission. This is the only way a flight crew, a team, or a working group can function at their very best. This is how you learn, how you expand, how you grow. And this is the fuel that allows ordinary people to come together to do extraordinary things as a single, clear-sighted, cohesive unit.

This is a strategic, purposeful decision. It does not happen randomly. Trust must be established and nurtured within a group; it's the only way we can ensure consistently high performance and enduring success.

A flight crew is a single entity, united in purpose, intention, and direction. It is not just a group of people working together.

It is many people coming together, flying as one.

8

PREPARE FOR HEADWINDS

IF I WERE ASKED TO CHOOSE an aircraft to fly into the face of persistent, driving winds, for hours straight, across thousands of miles, I'd want something nimble and powerful. This would be no time for the Cessna 172 from my first flight lesson, because I know the harder the winds blow, the more power we must bring to counter their force. In my best-case scenario, I would choose one equipped with the ability to refuel midair, extending my journey as long as need be.

To tackle this mission at my best, I'd take the controls of a fighter jet.

Just as quickly as blue skies can turn black, the direction of life's changing winds can impact how and when we reach our destinations. Relentless headwinds can feel insurmountable, testing our energy as we charge forward. But the better prepared we are to manage these outside forces when we're in their midst—and to anticipate their arrival to the extent that we can—the more freedom, joy, and sense of personal control we will discover within the spaces of our daily lives.

It's important to remember that headwinds and turbulence are not the same thing. When you hear the word *turbulence*, I want you to think of a *sudden change*. Air moving in all directions can cause a plane to suddenly lose or gain altitude and when it's extreme enough, can even cause structural damage. However, headwinds, tailwinds, and crosswinds often arrive as *weather systems*—air masses capable of spanning thousands of miles, across land and sea. In this Flight Lesson, we are focusing specifically on headwinds—the winds that not only slow us down but also drain our fuel tanks dry. The good news here—the silver lining—is that while *life's* turbulence often shows up with a sudden bang, headwinds can be planned for, intelligently strategized, and most importantly, faced (and flown through) with courage and determination.

The fury of life's headwinds originates in many forms: The loss of a loved one can suddenly leave us flying solo. The arrival of a pink slip can force us to rework our entire flight plan. Strong, persistent headwinds like this are capable of dashing dreams, but in most cases, even when the crisis hits suddenly, like turbulence, we grip the controls tightly, navigate our way through, and we *figure it out*. Survival instincts kick in. But the insidious power of a headwind lies in its ability to run our tanks dry slowly and steadily.

Those who make it through, who have hunkered down and considered all viable options, face opposing forces with tenacity and unshakeable determination. We may not enjoy this kind of flying in the moment, but headwinds inspire the kind of growth that changes us for the better. In headwinds, we discover our true character.

In this Flight Lesson, we will learn that flying head-on into these winds is not our only option. Flight training has taught me that we have several viable alternatives at our disposal, probably more than we realize. To exercise these options requires both awareness and a willingness to explore and expand. However you decide to navigate these challenges in your life, cling fast to the knowledge that you will not only get through . . . you will get through stronger. Wiser. More resilient. Better prepared to face the next challenge that comes your way. *Growth will always occur.*

Life itself is comprised of opposites, with all the potential to swing us wildly between forces, eventually yielding to one other to create a final balance that is unique within each of us. Just as headwinds are relative to the strength of the plane flying into them, each of us feels the force of headwinds at different levels of intensity. What feels like just a strong breeze to you may be someone else's insurmountable gale-force wind.

Exercise your options

Pilots use high-altitude wind charts to understand the weather environment they plan to fly into. These charts do not predict local weather events, but rather they illuminate the big picture. These charts let us know if we need to

90   prepare for, say, a ten-hour flight that includes twenty-knot or two-hundred-knot winds. This knowledge gives us precious time to evaluate the intensity of upcoming headwinds, and to the extent that we can, anyway, to develop a rational and dispassionate response to their arrival. With this knowledge, we're less likely to be caught off guard, knocked off-balance. While you cannot control the intensity or duration of a headwind, you *can* control subtle aspects of how you choose to withstand its force. Know that this control belongs to you, and let this awareness give you strength—and hope.

Remember when I mentioned that headwinds are *relative?* This means the lighter the plane, the less headwind that plane can withstand. Weight is important; along with a strong engine, it is what allows the plane to counter the opposing force of the headwind itself. Think of yourself through the years, once resembling a light and susceptible training aircraft easily blown back by the winds in your younger years, but eventually maturing and learning to respond to those winds with the force of a fighter jet—nimble, aerodynamic, not invincible but pretty darn close. This translates to growth, maturation, resilience.

This strength, this sense of solidity and balance, comes with age, and let me be clear: I'm still developing my own. These muscles grow stronger over time while we are simply living our lives. The passage of time and experience itself bring about a transition of sorts. When we are relatively young and facing our first headwinds—the college student who must work two jobs to pay for tuition, for instance, or the young, single mother struggling to pay for daycare and feed her family at the same time—it is more difficult to withstand the winds; we feel as if we don't have enough weight to face the winds.

What if I told you I could fly an aircraft in the same exact direction, to the same exact destination, with not just a lessened headwind but, in some cases, the helpful push of a tailwind? It's true. Changes in altitude can place us in much more favorable conditions. All it takes to gain access to this friendly environment is a call to air traffic control stating what you need to make it to your destination.

People often miss this parallel here on the ground because they have been brought up to believe that suffering through the storm is the most "heroic" pursuit or because they simply haven't yet learned to trust themselves to get on the radio and communicate precisely what they need. But these slight adjustments and course corrections—these imaginative, creative alternatives—are waiting to be explored. We should let go of the idea that hunkering down equates to heroism and instead consider a version of a hero who bravely explores all the options and tools at her disposal and chooses the response that best suits *her strategy*.

This is why pilots are constantly adjusting their altitude—to find the "sweet spot" above or below the strongest headwinds. Even a minor tweak can sometimes make a major difference: increase or decrease your altitude by a few thousand feet, for instance, and you'll face less resistance, be able to reassess and calculate your *new* fuel burn, and ultimately extend the range within which you'll be capable of flying. These subtle but in some cases lifesaving adjustments are not "one and done" but rather will require our attention throughout the course of all the flights we make, because trying new things means we're operating in new and evolving conditions.

You, too, can make these kinds of adjustments in your own life. Instead of accepting the prolonged and painful grief of losing your loved one and embracing this pain as your "new normal," the time may come when grief counseling provides the empathetic tailwind you'd almost forgotten existed. Or turning to a close friend for comfort after you've sustained a serious mental or emotional blow. *It is within your power to seek and find a different altitude that will lessen the intensity of your pain.* This is easy to forget when you are in the throes of crisis and chaos, when you feel powerless and overwhelmed and are weary of expending such effort. Let me remind you again: Even during the most severe headwinds, it is within your power to decide how to react. There are choices and they belong to you.

To explore all the options before us, however, requires a willingness to expand beyond our traditional ways of thinking—a shift in our mindset. Such a shift can feel seismic, but we must trust ourselves enough to yield to such positive new growth. We must be willing to ask for guidance. Just as I trusted air traffic control to direct me to more favorable airspace during the most intense moments of all sixteen legs of my around-the-world flight, I urge you, too, to reach out to the experts in your life who have the undeniable advantage of an outside perspective: therapists, mentors, close friends, and the *new* experts you will inevitably discover through serendipity and circumstance and even search engines.

By intelligently lightening our emotional load, we give ourselves headspace to be more creative, more imaginative, and, occasionally, even more boldly audacious in how we explore new ways to navigate our headwinds. Amid chaos and confusion, always try to operate from a place of emotional clarity and rational understanding. Remain vitally aware of the fact that you are not trying to lessen the intensity of the winds themselves—*no one* can do that—but simply adjusting (and optimizing) the conditions of your flight.

Also understand that even the slightest course corrections require intensity of focus, thoughtful preparation, and awareness of the resulting consequences. Up in the sky, if I decide to drop my altitude by, say, a few thousand feet to remove myself from a headwind, I might very well be putting myself into the crosshairs of a crosswind, which will only push me further off course! We must intentionally choose how we angle ourselves into the wind. Developing this sense of discernment is a learned skill; it exists within all of us, not just within a select few.

Accept helpful headwinds

Headwinds *of the right speed*, however, work in our favor. Think of the entrepreneur preparing to launch an exciting new product. Day one of the launch can certainly feel like flying into a headwind, as the world watches and waits, preparing to cast judgement upon your premiere takeoff. But the pure energy of the moment—that exhilarating moment of separation when the idea leaves the ground and takes *flight*—far outweighs the accompanying anxiety and uncertainty. That first moment of takeoff—the launch—is always the most powerful moment of the entire flight, simply because it is filled with such potential and so much transformative energy. This is why our greatest pursuits can make us feel, especially in that precious, powerful moment of liftoff, like we can defy gravity. I know they have for me.

In the cockpit, the moment of takeoff requires full attention from the pilot, and all the energy the engine has to offer. How we begin each flight at that moment of takeoff sets the tone for our entire journey! In life, that moment of "liftoff" is also when we need our enthusiasm, our energy level, and our commitment to be the most intense. Use this extraordinarily powerful energy; let it propel you forward. Don't be afraid of the headwinds. *Just get up there.* You can figure out how to navigate the oncoming winds once you are aloft. This isn't reckless; it's precise. You must not let the runway become a permanent parking space for your dreams.

Let's get specific: I've always been an early riser. Waking before sunrise just works for me. My body and mind seem to naturally want to *create* at this time of day. Ask me to change the world at eight o'clock in the evening, and I will give it my best, but I'd tackle the task with *much* more focus and intensity in those peaceful, pre-dawn hours. So, find your most comfortable creative space—the space where you can breathe and simply *be*—and commit to spending a little more time there. Whether that space is under the sun or the stars, this is sacred space, simply because it belongs to you.

During my around-the-world flight, I brought a favorite T-shirt that reads, "Get up an hour earlier to live an hour longer." I like that I know when I operate at my best; it makes working more enjoyable and it allows me to face my challenges with energy, enthusiasm, and intention, even (perhaps *especially*) during the strongest of headwinds.

A quick list to carry you through

I want to bring this chapter to a close by infusing it with a forward-moving, solution-driven momentum. Leaving you with this quick list of tips and suggestions on how to face your headwinds will hopefully give you the lift you need to pull away from the ground and just *get up there*. Only once you take off can you gain access to the navigational strategies just waiting for you above.

Ask for help. Flying into strong, sustaining headwinds is *real work*. Just as each airplane flies with a finite amount of fuel on board, so, too, do we. If we insist upon running our tank dry in flight, all the fuel in the world can't help us out if it's way down there on the ground. Draining our own personal fuel tanks can also drain us of our resolve, tricking us into thinking we are isolated and alone on our journey. Let this chapter be a reminder that you never *have* to be alone. You can always reach out to bring a trusted copilot or flight crew member on board. This means going to the boss and admitting you're having a hard day and could really use the extra space of a longer break, or turning to a family member or close friend and simply saying, "Mind taking the controls for a moment? I know it is not like me, but right now, I could use a break." Turn to those who have already flown through storms of similar intensity, not just for comfort but for strength, guidance, and direction.

It was my own flight instructors, from the earliest lessons all the way through my commercial exam, who drilled in the constant reminder that when headwinds arrive, I always have the option to explore adjusting my altitude.

"Air traffic control, this is Pilatus Five Eight November Golf, we're up against some pretty strong headwinds. Would you mind advising on a more favorable altitude for us to cruise?"

"Pilatus Five Eight November Golf, affirmative. Standby for further clearance."

It can really be as simple as that.

Create pockets of peace. In the midst of crisis, it is important to create tiny pockets of peace and quiet respite whenever you possibly can. Be gentle with yourself. I want to be careful not to trivialize these momentary reprieves. These peaceful moments involve more than just lighting a candle and slipping into a bubble bath but rather, they are intentional spaces that you create to simply *breathe*. To recalibrate your thoughts and find your focus. To remind yourself that headwinds do not last forever and *how* you get there has a lot to do with how you feel once you arrive.

Cultivate your creativity. No type of creative expression is off limits when I need to find relief from headwinds. Here, anything goes; no answers are wrong; no answers are right. By embracing *all* that I am, by cultivating sides of myself I didn't even know were there, I immediately expand my field of vision. Through unselfconscious artistic expression, I've been guided to some of my most tangible and sophisticated real-world solutions.

Remember that others will learn from your logbook of life. As I write this book, we are in the middle of a global pandemic; it's a horrible headwind that has taken the lives of hundreds of thousands and has forced us to literally separate and physically isolate from each other. But take heart. Even in the midst of all this, we still have the wherewithal and the resources to explore different altitudes. We have the technology to connect with each other and the emotional, mental, and spiritual resilience to fly through this. We've been told not only that headwinds are present at all altitudes but that they will also remain strong for an unknown amount of time. One of the rare, but dazzling, silver linings as we live through this pandemic has been witnessing the global reliance, empathy, and compassion we've created among one another.

The lessons that we learn from these difficult moments, the wisdom that we glean, the enduring moments, and the new altitudes that we navigate will accumulate as meaningful entries in our logbook of life. And these are the headwinds that will ultimately make us strongest.

How we face our headwinds, how we decide to navigate the challenges and turmoil that threaten to slow us down and knock us off course will be the ultimate measure of our growth. We're not measuring ourself against someone else but against our own potential to do our best.

Through it all, remember that every headwind must eventually subside. And when it does, we will emerge stronger, more resilient, and more fully enlightened than we ever thought possible. Each experience will add more weight and balance to our journey. We will grow, mature, and evolve. And we will fly forward with the will and the determination to manage the new headwinds that are coming our way.

Next time you feel those headwinds start to blow, I urge you to swiftly take the controls. And don't be a Cessna.

Be a fighter jet.

NAVIGATE WITH INTENTION

IT'S FAIR TO SAY that if you're reading this book, venturing down "the road not taken" when in pursuit of a life goal is a path you've at least considered, if not taken. Robert Frost, in his well-known poem of the same title, writes that taking the road less traveled "has made all the difference." I couldn't agree more. When given the choice between a well-paved, familiar highway and an unfamiliar, twisting trail, it's not out of character for me to grab my trusty flashlight and head into the woods with the same enthusiasm Frost describes. Where is the adventure, excitement, and growth in taking a road that has already been traveled by so many others?

The paths we choose can determine the course of our trajectory, but they also offer an important glimpse into *how* we choose to travel through life. If we take the wide, multi-lane freeway that offers a straight path toward our destination, that same path might also be crowded and clogged with traffic but if we explore the "road not taken," the road with a few more twists and turns, we may set ourselves up for a more adventurous journey, with a more expansive, elevated view. Which path would you take?

In this moment, imagine yourself standing at that split in the road, each path representing a different but *viable* solution to a problem you're currently facing or have faced in the past. To your left, you see a well-lit, smoothly paved road; one you've probably traveled before. To your right lies a mysterious trail, overgrown with vines and while it sure is alluring, it also looks like only a few have trod in that direction before.

This split in the road feels constricting to me: Take the corporate job or live as a starving artist? Travel the world or buy a home and settle down? Operate within the world as a creative or as a mechanical, logical thinker? Here's the thing: I'm not interested in living such a black-and-white, either-or life. I want to sample a little bit of *everything*, to explore whichever path allows me to simply *be myself* in the world. I want more than just the either-or options. Why? Because there's so much more to life than either-or propositions. Life is multi-textured, multidimensional, and multidirectional. Why not explore it all?

Perhaps you've felt that same longing for more paths to pursue. While you're familiar with traditional options for life and career, maybe it feels like there's something out there more suited to you specifically. This feeling, reminding me I was not *meant* to navigate through this world along mostly traditional paths, is something I can recognize from childhood, and it remains today. Here, I want to share a deeply personal, methodical, and highly effective decision-making technique I've come to rely upon when seeking personal understanding and clarity before navigating toward my next direction of flight. I invite you to try it, too.

Navigating from the center of your compass

In this exercise, we need the freedom that comes from going airborne. Up above, there are no roads to follow; while there are certainly plenty of rules, this elevated perspective gives us the freedom to explore the vast 360 degrees of sky we now occupy.

Before I lead you step-by-step through this exercise, it's important to understand some basics about—the compass—the tool we'll be using as the main reference point for decisions.

Picture a standard magnetic handheld compass, the same kind you'd find at a sporting-goods store or in a basic outdoor emergency kit. According to *Encyclopedia Britannica*, the compass dates to the twelfth century, when mariners discovered that by placing a small sliver of magnetic ore on a piece of floating wood in still water, the ore would automatically align with the North Star. Therefore, when changing the direction you're facing while holding a magnetic compass of similar design, the magnetic needle remains pointed north and south.

To this day, most aircraft display a traditional magnetic compass in a prominent location in the cockpit. In an emergency, the compass can quickly become the best reference for pilots who simply want to know which way they are going. While more sophisticated navigational tools now provide insight into our physical location, from radar, to modern-day, satellite-based GPS, the compass will always remain. It's hard to argue with a metal needle that never fails to find its way back home.

Now that we're familiar on the basic science behind why a compass is such a reliable tool with which to navigate, it's time to begin building *your personal compass* I hope you'll turn to when a change in the direction of your life is necessary. On the ground, without the benefit of an elevated perspective that allows us look down and see what's below us and what's coming (both the dangers and the gifts) our vision is somewhat restricted. All we can see before us is that restrictive "fork in the road" choice. This way or that, left or right. But this simple exercise will allow us to elevate and expand our vision *while remaining here on the ground*. Compass in hand, we will be able to take a panoramic view of all the 360 directions we may choose to travel.

Step 1: Grab a sheet of blank paper and a pencil or pen. Draw a circle about the size of the base of your coffee cup. At the center of the circle, draw a point.

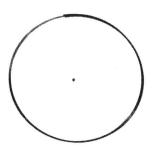

Step 2: Assuming North is the top of our sheet of paper, we'll label what are called the four *cardinal directions*, including north, south, east and west. *Merriam-Webster* states, "*Cardinal* goes back to the Latin adjective *cardinalis*, which meant 'serving as a hinge,'" later evolving "to mean 'something on which a development turns.'"

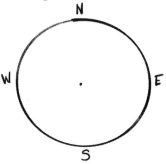

I share this information not to overwhelm you or complicate things, but to add meaning to your understanding of *your personal compass*. The four cardinal directions, equally spaced 90 degrees apart from one another, are most likely the first that come to mind when imagining directions on a compass. It's important to note that at this point in the exercise, we're only drawing our compass face, not the magnetic needle.

Step 3: On each of your cardinal directions, we'll begin to list the most common, well-known, and general ways to get to the goal you hope to reach. I used this exercise back when I was trying to figure out how best to pay for my flight lessons, a significant expense for a college student. This is the example we'll use throughout the exercise, because it certainly worked for me. My ultimate goal, then, was to "learn to fly on a budget," so I listed the four most obvious paths *first*.

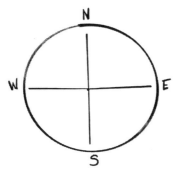

Step 4: We'll begin listing the next four options to reach our goal; these are our *ordinal directions*: northwest, southwest, northeast, and southeast. *Ordinal*, Latin for *order*, is the word describing the halfway point between each of the cardinal directions. Here, I want you to begin listing ways to reach your goal that are unusual, outlandish, unlikely . . . *but not impossible.*

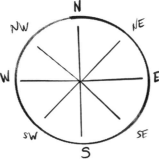

As you can clearly see, each unique heading on our compass represents a viable pathway out there in the world—a turn we can make, an adjustment from our current course that offers us another way to reach our goal. The goal itself does not change; *what changes is the path we decide to take to get there.*

Let's navigate through the challenge I faced in my early twenties: I wanted desperately to become a pilot, but my bank account was empty. Because my will to reach my destination was strong, I began listing out options. If I really, I mean *really*, wanted to learn how to fly, how could I get there? That's why we begin with our cardinal directions.

Ask yourself the question, "How would the average person out there in the world go about . . . ?" then simply fill in the blank with *your goal*. Once we move to the next level, the ordinal directions, you'll notice immediately that it's a lot harder to even list these options, let alone commit to them. If they don't come immediately to mind, that's okay. Be patient with the process and gentle with yourself. Understand that this is where you need to draw on more imaginative solutions so this might take a little more time.

Some options you list on your compass will reveal their natural inverse. I'll use my flight-training goal again to explain what I mean. When weighing the options between taking a military route to become a pilot and taking a bank loan, one felt more like saving and the other felt more like spending. It felt the same when I weighed the options between saving up slowly and immediately changing my major; one felt a bit like I'd be *paying* to fly; the other (becoming a pilot) would mean I'd someday get *paid* to fly. Taking the military route would involve a multiyear commitment, a bank loan comes with interest rates, and so on. Each option carried with it a resulting consequence of some kind. Listing multiple pathways helped elevate my perspective to see what I couldn't see if I'd simply taken the straight and narrow path. It allowed me to visually consider these consequences and the long-term navigational impacts of my decisions.

Take another look at your compass. With your eight newly illuminated routes—the star bursting out from the center of your compass, within which, remember, you have placed yourself—I want you to take pride in how simply and quickly you have quadrupled your options. From our original, abstract goal, we've now created eight actionable ways to move forward . . . and now, *we* decide we are ready.

Reclaiming true north

You may have noticed we never placed any special emphasis or marker signifying *true north* on our compass. That's because I left it off intentionally. I omitted it deliberately to signify that each direction on your compass holds significance and value. Just as the compass itself needs no special inscription or any prompting from us to indicate the direction we're heading—remember, it relies on its *own magnetic forces*—neither will we require outside validation or special prompting to know when we are on our right path. It will feel like an instant, innate connection you cannot deny; one I hope you associate with the multiple headings on your unique compass. *All* these headings—all of these new options and different paths—belong to you. Be confident and courageous enough to explore any of them.

I want you to trust yourself enough to be able to explore all these different directions, to at least be aware that they *exist*. This awareness is vital. The less we explore, the fewer headings we fly, the more restrictive our options become. This is when we shrink the number of paths available to us, an unfortunate and completely avoidable choice. If I can't even *visualize* a new heading on my compass, if I am so fearful of even the *idea* of moving within this undefined airspace, I am far less likely to continue moving forward, which might bring all momentum to a halt. This doesn't have to happen. This is why it is so important to maintain the momentum of your intentional drive. Find the course that is best for you, regardless of what others (usually those who only rely on their cardinal directions) have to say.

While our exercise here in the book takes us to eight headings, my hope is that you continue segmenting your compass until all 360 degrees are explored.

The infinite nature of your compass

Beyond just appreciating the simple function of this exercise, I hope you also begin to realize the power in the overarching theme of this chapter: *you can change your direction of flight any time you choose* by giving your compass an infinite number of headings from which to choose. I'm not condoning haphazard, random course corrections, but rather, keeping the freedom to change your course close at hand, in your back pocket, to explore as an option when the time is right. Will there be consequences and tradeoffs to changing course? Of course. Headwinds, tailwinds, turbulence, storms of all kinds will attempt to push you back onto those well-traveled headings that feel more familiar and might be easier to control. I urge you to do your best to stick it out, to follow whatever direction pulls you magnetically, even when you can't see more than a few miles ahead. Trust your inner compass.

Only by trusting your own inner guidance, at that magnetized, subconscious level—much like the pilot who's lost

her engine must rely on her compass to guide her to a safe 107
landing—can we fly through this life with confidence and
clarity. We can *learn* to trust our "inner guide," Remember,
this is an acquired skill and the more we do, the more we'll
come to learn far more about ourselves by the navigational
turns and the course corrections we make along the way.
Reducing our most complicated and meaningful life decisions to two paths—an easy street or a jagged cliff—is far
too simplistic for those who want to fully and wholeheartedly explore where they could end up next.

In what exciting new directions will your "road not taken"
lead you next?

10

PROTECT YOUR WEIGHT AND BALANCE

FOR EVERY AIRPLANE, there exists a completely unique, predetermined formula that determines the amount of weight that plane can safely carry and how that weight should be distributed and arranged. The goal is to balance what we carry around a center point or, in this case, our center of gravity. From the moment the plane begins taxiing toward the runway, however, a minuscule shifting of both weight and balance has already begun. These fluctuations are constant, and they are inevitable.

These fluctuations are why weight and balance requirements are based on an acceptable *range*, rather than on a precise number. As we fly, we burn fuel. The same is true on the ground: though we must certainly strive to keep our lives balanced, *perfect balance at all times* is impossible.

This Flight Lesson is about standing up for personal limits, respecting boundaries, and discovering that the pilot in command is responsible for what is loaded onto their plane.

One indisputable fact is that our lives, priorities, and interests are constantly shifting. Responsibilities, emotions, obligations all symbolize cargo, which must be arranged and rearranged amid the obligations, commitments, and objects we're already carrying. Just as each pilot is responsible for computing an aircraft's weight and balance calculation for each flight, on the ground this responsibility to find our unique balance also belongs to us.

In this Flight Lesson, we will give ourselves permission to manage and adjust the things we decide to bring (and keep) on board our daily journey. We won't really focus on *what* we bring on board, but more on *how we choose to carry the load*. This is going to take a brave and brutally honest inventory of what we've allowed on our plane.

Is our current cargo weighing us down in a way that pushes us off-course and prevents us from reaching our destination as efficiently as possible? If that's the case, are we able to make the necessary adjustments to establish a more manageable balance? Let's look at an example: You've recently received an unpleasant diagnosis from your doctor that has added new weight and worry to your life. Things feel understandably off-balance. What will you do to right this load? Will you figure out a way to redistribute this new cargo and process this new information so that your anxiety doesn't blow you off-course? When we lean too far outside of our acceptable weight and range requirements, we need to act with a sense of urgency and dispatch to restore balance to our flight.

So, you might decide to rise an hour earlier every day to walk, meditate, or take that new yoga class you've been considering. This involves logical, clear-sighted, solution-driven thinking on your part, combined with the will and determination to follow up with intentional action. *Alter your schedule. Shift some things around to establish a new balance, then commit to maintaining this healthy new balance. Don't get distracted. Remember that you are the pilot in command of this new flight toward renewed strength and recovery. How you choose to carry this weight can literally shorten or extend how long you'll be able to stay in flight.*

Part of adjusting the emotional weight we carry with us moving forward requires us to take a long, honest look at how (and what) we've brought with us from the past. Being able to adjust this weight—to rid ourselves of the burdens that have weighed us down from as far back as our childhood—is an important part of this process. Here, I'll use myself as an example.

Being Amelia: the childhood challenges

Before I write another word, I want to stop for a moment to give my childhood self—the loving, lovely, ten-year-old Amelia Rose I was back in grade school—a warm hug and a gentle pat on the little back. I want to look her in the eye and

tell her how proud I am of her for carrying all the weight she
carried on her little-girl shoulders.

I also want to say that my mom and dad loved me deeply; I know their intention was for this name to give me wings to fly. Today, I can give space for the possibility they didn't realize that naming their daughter Amelia Earhart would place such a heavy weight on their little girl's shoulders. They both tell me they simply hoped the name would prove to be a source of motivation and inspiration; so the decision itself came from a place of love.

I don't think they realized, back then, that their own reluctance to explore whether there was a biological relationship with Amelia (much less confirm it, which they couldn't) only added to that unwanted weight. They didn't know that the *not* knowing, the uncertainty, the doubt surrounding this unanswered question would leave me feeling anxious, isolated, vulnerable, and afraid until my early thirties. I shifted and adjusted that weight by trying to live up to the expectations of others. I tried to be pleasant, polite, obedient, and kind. But what I want to say to that little girl now is, *"I am proud of you for withstanding the pressure. You were doing the very best that you could. That's a massive weight for anyone to carry."*

I was a good kid, what my Mom calls an "easy child." I studied hard. I was kind and caring toward others. But the expectations and the constant inquiries from others—"Aren't you going to be a pilot when you grow up so you can be like the *real* Amelia Earhart?"—weighed me down and left me feeling imbalanced and untethered. From as early as I can remember, I simply didn't know how to offload that burden; I didn't have the capacity. I just assumed the burden belonged to me and darn it, I was going to be the best Amelia Earhart I could possibly be, no matter what. I didn't want to disappoint anyone. Adults made it clear I was to honor Amelia's important legacy, too. It was a lot of weight to carry with my then tiny wings.

There was someone in my young life, though, who helped redistribute some of the weight that was pressing down on my little shoulders. Mrs. Ramsey, my second-grade teacher, was one of the first adults in my life to embrace me for simply being me. She also helped me learn to celebrate the fact that it was amazing to be named after a trailblazer in aviation history, whether I decided to follow in her footsteps or not.

Every month, sweet, gentle, bespectacled Mrs. Ramsey would assign a student the distinguished status of being classroom "VIP"—a high honor, indeed. The little student of distinction would sit at the front of the classroom, in a chair emblazoned with a fabric covering with the letters "VIP" in a worn and faded blue-and-white striped fabric—custom-made by Mrs. Ramsey herself. The "VIP" also had special duties and responsibilities, reading the lunch menu aloud, reading attendance, and acting as line leader. Being classroom "VIP" meant you were also the closest copilot to our beloved Mrs. Ramsey.

When it came my turn to be "VIP," I'll always remember how Mrs. Ramsey coordinated a special "Amelia Earhart Week" so that the entire class could study the life of the great aviator. This intuitive, inspired teacher clearly sensed how much weight the name placed on me; she saw me being teased and cajoled by the other kids and she must have sensed how much it stung.

It was Mrs. Ramsey who first taught me, and the entire second-grade class, that Amelia Earhart was not just an extraordinary pilot, but that she'd also been a social worker, a fashion and luggage designer and a photographer. It was Mrs. Ramsey who opened my eyes to the splendid *fullness* of Amelia Earhart—inviting me for the first time, to let go of the burden of the name, and replace it with an invitation to fly in any direction I'd choose.

Still, though, I ended up bringing much of that burden with me into adulthood. My driving desire to live up to other people's expectations, my fear of disappointing others, the anxiety that came from not knowing whether there was a biological relationship—all these added weight to my journey into adulthood. Still, I'm certain that burden was made lighter by Mrs. Ramsey's compassion and creativity. Today, I've managed to let go of nearly all the weight that my childhood Amelia had to bear. There are vestiges that remain, certainly, but here and now I want to open my cargo hold and release myself of those last few vestiges—and what better a place to do it than here, in this chapter on managing what we hold onto and what we release. To my little-girl self who still lives within me: *I release you of those weights and burdens; I drop them into the swirling sea beneath me.*

You can do this, too. Face the weights and burdens of your past openly and honestly; this is what will give you the energy and the will necessary to push them overboard, once and for all.

It's funny, but whenever I picture Mrs. Ramsey today, I *still* picture myself looking up at her from my child-like, second-grade perspective.

And I still look up to her.

114 Saving space for me

It took me a long time to learn how to use the word "No." For much of my early life, "Yes" was my default response. Whenever an aviation-related invitation came my way, my mind flooded with what I imagined I'd hear back, "Your name's *Amelia Earhart* . . . you should probably be here, *don't you think?*" A few times, that's exactly what I heard back. So, I went.

How could I say "no" to representing Amelia? Was I not proud of my name? The invitations often came from earnest, well-meaning organizations. However over time, I came to realize that it was far more important, and far more fulfilling, to say "yes" to the projects and possibilities that were close to my heart and more directly aligned with my goals, dreams, and interests. This required an intentional shift in mindset on my part. I made a purposeful decision to redistribute the cargo on my own flight in a way that ensured I reach my ultimate destination as Amelia *Rose*—whatever that destination happened to be—*even if it meant disappointing others.*

Conceptualizing and planning my around-the-world flight certainly helped facilitate this process. If I was going to get this flight off the ground, in both a literal and a figurate sense, I needed to devote full focus to every conceivable aspect of the journey, which required every ounce of energy, fortitude, and determination I had within me. It *made* me realign my priorities.

I think back to that stage in my life; I was waking up around three a.m. each morning for my TV news career, still readily accepting invitations from every club, every board, and every aviation charity event, large or small, near or far.

I was beginning to plan my around-the-world flight, burning the candle at both ends, trying to please everyone. I finally had to redistribute and rebalance the weight of all that I was carrying; but I had to do more than re-balance. I had to off-load, too.

This is when I began using the word "No" more frequently. If this flight was going to be truly successful, I needed to ascribe to it a new value: Highest priority, which only I could assign. Each aspect of planning was critical: Initiating and securing corporate support. Creating and curating a website, fundraising for my foundation, building an authentic "brand" around the flight itself. Spending more hours in the sky, conducting test flights, building my technical expertise, becoming the very best pilot I could possibly be in preparation for the flight.

This level of focus *required* me to learn to say, "No." I learned to evaluate, prioritize, and assess quickly if each trip, presentation or speech would propel me closer to my goals. This new clarity of thought and this new awareness that I needed to adjust the weight and balance in my life in a way that ensured the ultimate success of my flight.

I began *telling* people clearly, respectfully—and this is important, without apology—that planning my around-the-world flight was my highest priority, and that this was going to *remain* my focus until the mission had been accomplished. I knew that if I ran my inner fuel tank dry flying to everyone else's destinations, I'd never reach my own.

We must *own* and understand the impact weight and balance has on how we fly; we are accountable for the weight we carry—and we must be responsible for lessening our load, or redistributing the weight we carry. The mother of three, for instance, who might feel overwhelmed, anxious,

116 and resentful about having to bear the constant weight of playing the role of homework helper, the meal organizer, and the household peacekeeper has the right to evaluate, and continually reevaluate how she can redistribute her personal balance.

Take pride in your priorities, re-set them when you have to, then communicate these principles, practices, and priorities to those around you without apology. Trust me: Most people will appreciate (and perhaps even admire) your honesty. I've even been told my learned ability to say, "No," has inspired others how to do the same, and for that I am proud.

Today, I no longer manage the expectations of others, but I continue to assign and hold lofty expectations for myself. This has freed up precious cargo space where I now on board whatever new cargo, whatever new projects, ideas, and commitments I have joyfully and intentionally chosen to take on.

Treat each new day as a new flight

We already know that *no* plane remains in complete balance and at a constant weight throughout the flight. It's impossible. With this knowledge, we create acceptable ranges within which we can comfortably work. We can do this on the ground, too. We must always be able to account and adjust for changing variables. Knowing that we can carry up to a certain amount, but at some point, taking on more weight puts us in actual danger.

A quick morning assessment of my personal weight and balance arrangement reminds me that each day is a brand-new flight. I don't have to carry yesterday's burdens into today's journey. Just as every takeoff and every flight is new and will never be experienced again, so, too, is how you fill your day. You are allowed to leave your cargo space open for new possibilities and opportunities for growth, expansion, and discovery. That you are in complete control of navigating your day, determining its balance, adjusting your schedule, is a powerful and very practical piece of absolute knowledge. Each new day, each new *minute*, belongs to you.

Try to let this fresh, new, minute-by-minute awareness provide forgiving buoyancy and balance to every day. Fly your plane and balance your cargo as efficiently as you can; just as each aircraft in operation has a completely unique weight and balance calculation, so do you. Unpack that old cargo that you've been carrying—dusty boxes crammed with old fears, outdated resentments, stale ideas, stagnant relationships, childhood traumas—and leave them on the ground below. For me, therapy, trial and error, self-acceptance, and simply growth have helped me learn to communicate clearly and openly with others. Just because someone near you offloads her burdens, does not mean you are responsible for picking the person up. Instead, speak up.

Several years ago, after a minor disagreement with a dear friend, we began communicating less frequently, both of us awkwardly avoiding the simple conversation that could quickly clear the air. From there, life went on and it wasn't until almost a year later that I reluctantly reached out to call her. Worried there might still be resentment or anger between us, I had worked myself into an anxious mess, creating stories in my head of all the angry ways she'd reject my attempt to connect. Happier to hear her friend's voice than upset over our petty misunderstanding, we both admitted that we'd been carrying around that emotional weight for an entire year. One call made both our flights lighter and more fun to fly.

When the weight you're carrying feels too heavy, clear up confusion by opening the boxes you've shoved in the back of your plane. Don't let the weight of resentment and anger become dusty, useless baggage on your precious and limited lifetime of flight. Resentments can get greedy; they are always eager to take up space. Don't let them. Be empowered to ditch unnecessary cargo. Be precise about what you pack on board *each flight, every day* and be precise about what you choose to leave behind on the ground. Now it's time to enjoy your flight, unimpeded, imperfectly balanced but adjusting all the time, newly free to explore all the beauty we can store in its place.

11

RESPECT THE HOLDING PATTERN

EVERY AVIATOR KNOWS the shortest distance between two airports is a straight line of flight, which is why I've never met another pilot who enjoys or looks forward to circling in a holding pattern. This tried-and-true maneuver takes our flight plan and *throws it out the window*, because in this situation, it's no longer just about us and our specific flight: holding patterns are designed to protect *everyone* within the airspace we've agreed to fly within.

120   When air traffic control orders a pilot to assume and maintain a holding pattern (a predetermined, oval-shaped course flown by aircraft waiting to receive further clearance in a specific airspace), immediate and total adherence is not only necessary but mandatory. Holding patterns are specifically designed to keep aircraft safely separated and organized in the air while the crews on the ground deal with whatever unanticipated challenge is at hand, with the goal, of course, being the safe and methodical landing of every plane.

Air traffic controllers have the technology and the capacity to see what individual pilots cannot, whether it's a crash on the runway, an emergency landing, or a severe weather system that might be preventing other planes from landing safely. It is their *role* to see what the pilots in the sky cannot, particularly in times of crisis or severe weather, they are our eyes and ears. Air traffic control is the central authority, issuing both direction *and* directives, so when a holding pattern becomes necessary, collective adherence is necessary—for the safety of everyone involved.

One example of a real-world holding pattern we can all relate to is the coronavirus pandemic. When COVID-19 emerged and the world entered varying levels of shutdowns and restrictions, each of us were forced to limit the "airspace" in which we once operated. Our personal, social and work lives were suddenly reduced to a very small space—our homes—where we found ourselves circling, waiting for permission from the government to give us clearance to return to our normal lives. To protect one another from the spread of this rapidly spreading deadly virus, we hunkered down and waited to be given further clearance. During this time, emotions ran high, seemingly spanning the entire spectrum of human feelings, from frustration to grief to empathy and beyond.

It was in the first few weeks of the pandemic that I realized just how similar this feeling of being told to stay home was to being placed in a holding pattern by air traffic control. The flight path I'd been confidently flying was immediately brought to a halt, and suddenly I was circling in place, burning fuel, yet getting no closer toward my goals. I'd just started a new position at the TV station where I worked, purchased a new home, and was living alone. The isolation I felt was real and I often found myself wondering if I'd ever make it out of this confusing time.

It was only once I began shifting my perspective, in an attempt to see the big picture, that I could keep myself calm, gaining an understanding that I wasn't alone in my fear and lack of clarity. When I began to imagine myself on a radar screen, I could slowly zoom out. This exercise took me out of my individual emotions and reminded me that I wasn't alone. My neighbors, my city, my state, my country and ultimately, the world, were each in their own difficult and limiting holding pattern, experiencing the same feelings I was. When I placed myself in the context of the entire pandemic, I felt clarity and connection, and I realized I was a part of something much bigger than just me.

While I couldn't control when the pandemic would end and life would go back to normal, I could do my part to stop the spread of germs by limiting when I left the house. While I couldn't change the fact that I was suddenly working from home, broadcasting live from my living room with all the technical difficulties we each endured during this adjustment period, I could make the best of the experience, working creatively to do my best, given the circumstances. While I couldn't go out and be social with the ease of my pre-pandemic life, I could connect thoughtfully and intentionally with my friends and family through phone and video conversations.

This is what I mean when I say there is an art to navigating the holding pattern. The art is in choosing to operate with an attitude to do your best, even when the circumstances aren't ideal. Complaining about a holding pattern won't get you out of it any quicker, but seeing the big picture and doing our best when we are forced to endure challenges out of our control can be the difference maker.

It was during the COVID pandemic, with all the unexpected time at home forced upon all of us, that I decided it was time to get serious about writing this book. I finally had the time, the quiet, the focus and the introspection to devote the attention it deserved, and, as I look back, I'm so grateful that I used my time spent in this holding pattern to achieve a goal I'd been slowly working toward for years.

Sharing airspace

I've never encountered another pilot who looks forward to flying holding patterns. Being held back from our destination can facilitate feelings of frustration, resentment, and anger. But take heart: holding patterns do not last forever. A holding pattern is a temporary "state of being," designed to stabilize the environment until the crisis or challenge has been addressed, managed, and corrected.

During an emergency or a crisis—whether it's a severe weather system, a natural disaster, or a global pandemic—we must yield to a greater authority (pilots must yield to air traffic control; citizens must yield to the scientific and global health community) to help us navigate through. Order must be established, and everyone plays a vital role. Oversight is involved. There are new patterns, deliberately restrictive in their very nature, which must be observed until the crisis has been averted. For the greater good of all, each involved participant must take their role seriously. Noncompliance can bring serious, even fatal, consequences.

Becoming a pilot means agreeing to all the rules and regulations, not just the ones that are easy to follow. In cases of crisis and challenge, it's important to remember that everyone who is impacted (or potentially impacted) has a responsibility to uphold the greater good. The fact that we all *belong to each other* and are each responsible for ensuring one another's safety and well-being could be seen as a comforting, reassuring piece of knowledge rather than a burdensome obligation; it connects us more directly to each other, which is particularly important when so many of us are feeling isolated, set apart, and vulnerable.

This principle, this holding pattern, requires physical, emotional, and mental awareness and a sense of collective altruism. Again, it is a collective *state of being*. An attitude. A vital awareness. Holding patterns are not passive, benign systems that are designed to inconvenience us and cause us strife; they are necessary patterns designed to bring order to disorder, as serious in their intent as any emergency procedure. Failure to adhere means failure to uphold and protect the greater good.

It's also important to remember that when we are forced to remain in a holding pattern, whether it's the pilot circling just above LaGuardia, waiting for the signal from air traffic control that the plane has been cleared to land, or the driver stuck in a road closure due to hazardous conditions, we must remember that we are not operating alone. There is always the greater good to consider. This kind of collective behavior and respectful adherence to the rules—whatever "rules" those happen to be, in the air or on the ground—creates an intricate, interdependent web of accountability. We all play a role.

We must all face these mandatory (and unavoidable) holding patterns at some point in our lives. Learning to embrace them—learning to fly within this tightly constricted airspace—deepens the sense of collective responsibility that we feel toward one another and magnifies our sense of selflessness and belonging. It also requires patience, endurance, and the willingness to function as part of a larger, more fully integrated team.

Unlike the rest of this book, where I've repeatedly emphasized the importance of personal choice, personal empowerment, and exercising individual control of our daily lives, this chapter is a little different: Here, we emphasize collective accountability. Here, we recognize the vital importance of "taking one for the team" when the situation demands it. Here, the *me* becomes *we*. Holding patterns *should* have that kind of unifying effect.

Silver linings found in holding patterns

When forces out of our control keep us from flying toward our destination, knowing how to throttle back and reduce and maintain a predetermined, specific, and much slower speed is essential. There is an art to navigating the hold.

I practiced this art here on the ground during the planning phase of my around-the-world flight, as much of our coordination involved waiting for permission to move forward. Applying for permits. Acquiring visas. Seeking approval from the FAA. Obtaining overflight clearances. When I explain why this flight took two solid years of planning, these are the specific reasons why. These specific holding patterns I placed myself in were necessary, and mandatory, before the flight itself could commence. But all the waiting, all the holding in place I was required to endure never *once* made me feel impatient enough to want to abort or postpone the flight. If anything, it made me more determined to do whatever was needed to be done so that the flight could happen.

When Pilatus, the aircraft manufacturer, granted me permission to use its plane for the flight, it set my plan into motion with an undeniable momentum. With access to the right aircraft, I could exit this holding pattern, increase my speed once again, and fly forward by coordinating the correct corporate sponsors, applying for certain licenses and insurance, putting contracts in place, and a seemingly endless list of other mandatory requirements that demanded attention, clearances, and permission.

In fact, it's worth noting that this extended holding pattern was a vital and necessary part of the flight itself. Had I not remained within it, had I not done the things I needed to do—drafted the contracts I needed to contract, assembled the team I needed to assemble, obtained the permissions I needed to obtain—the trip would never have gotten off the ground. These are not the exciting and romantic aspects of my journey but without them, I never would have left the ground.

Holding patterns are not the time to let your guard down, just because you're stuck flying in circles in constricted airspace. Instead, use them to assess your situation; a confident pilot can exit the hold with a feeling of potential, power, and the promise of reaching new destinations and, yes, even freedom. Was I ready to exit that holding pattern once everything had been approved, obtained, and set into place? You better believe I was. I was ready to exit but, here's the important tiny nuance that holds an extraordinary distinction: I was also *prepared* to exit. I knew how to exit. So, in a very real way, all those extended holding patterns made taking off on that flight, that moment of separation from the ground, all the sweeter. We must remember in life, too, that knowing how to exit the holding pattern is as important as remaining within one. Both are acquired skills.

Don't go silent in the hold

What holding patterns are you flying within your own life right now? Are you waiting for your career to take a change in direction, perhaps? Or maybe waiting for that fresh, new relationship to blossom into a deeper level of commitment? You might even be in graduate school, waiting to push out into the world and make your mark as a professional. Wherever you are, and whatever holding pattern it is that you might be experiencing, take heart: holding patterns are purposeful periods of waiting. Use the time to grow. To deepen. To test your fortitude and polish up your relationship with patience.

While we are within these holding patterns,

however—whether you're being temporarily confined to the house because of poor health or you're waiting to receive news from a potential employer about whether they've decided to bring you on board—do not go silent. In fact, knowing when to reach out and establish communication with others, especially during difficult times, is an acquired skill that you will do well to hone. Direct, ongoing communication with others—a trusted family member or close friend, a therapist, a member of the clergy, a colleague at work—helps lessen the stress and fight the fatigue, and it makes you feel like a valued member of a larger team. Again, we are not islands.

Whether it's the pilot communicating with air traffic control to confirm the precise coordinates of his holding pattern or the young student taking a moment to simply pick up the phone to check in on her elderly, isolated relative, this kind of outreach carries with it a special significance during a time of crisis or emergency. If there's something distracting you, disturbing you, or creating an imbalance in your life, especially if it's exacerbated by having to "hold in place," you need to trust yourself enough to reach out to others and talk it through. It is vital to reach out to others, particularly during difficult times. Make that human connection.

In that same vein, I hope you recognize the importance of being able to let others know that *you* might be the one who needs a little extra attention; you might be feeling a little vulnerable, a little afraid, or just a little lonely because you're remaining in a holding pattern. It is incumbent upon you, then, to let your loved ones know you could really benefit from a phone call, a text, or a video visit. Trust yourself enough to say freely to the people you love, "You know, I'm having a little bit of difficulty staying in this holding pattern, and I might just need you to check in on me when you get a free moment, okay?"

The ultimate questions we should always ask ourselves are, "How can I make this person's time aloft a little more enjoyable? What can I do to ease some of the stress they're experiencing from having to remain in this holding pattern?" This altruistic thinking and behavior are both inspired and inspiring.

Holding patterns are a part of taking flight

The best pilots are the ones who know the rules, follow those rules, and adhere to those rules even (perhaps especially) during an in-flight emergency. This is what allows them to stay calm amid chaos. This is what allows them to remain in that mandatory holding pattern for as long as it takes, for as long as they're told, and for as long as is necessary to manage the issue at hand.

Next time you find yourself in a forced holding pattern, I'd encourage you to adapt a pilot-like attitude. Adhere to the rules and know that the situation can't last forever. Elevate your priorities and your perspective so that you are putting the greater good in mind. Keep your standards of behavior and accountability during this time as high as you would at any other point in your life—perhaps even higher. Don't be daunted by the holding pattern; be *energized* by it. And as long as you're in it, be the very best human being you can possibly be. This is the healthiest, most productive way to proceed . . . not just for you.

For all of us.

12

HARNESS YOUR TAILWINDS

PILOTS OFTEN JOKE that tailwinds, the winds traveling in the *same direction* as our aircraft rather than against it, are a bit like free fuel. Tailwinds get us to where we want to be faster *and* with less effort, so it's easy to see why pilots often rejoice in their presence. There is a good chance you've enjoyed this force already, that is, if you've ever heard your captain on a commercial flight announce an early arrival to your destination. Put simply, tailwinds are on our side.

And while we should certainly learn to appreciate these moments of added propulsion when they grace us with their presence, I also believe we can *create* tailwinds here on the ground by helping others reach their goals sooner and with just a little less effort. Here's the double-barreled beauty of a tailwind: it's great to receive one yourself but even greater to *create* one for someone else. Learn to do both and you benefit twice.

In this Flight Lesson, we'll learn how to propel others toward their destinations through tangible expressions of support, compassion, sharing, understanding, and in my case, of sisterhood. This Flight Lesson is about listening to what others need and finding ways we can help, and I consider it one of the most essential and meaningful themes of this book.

In the book's Introduction, I shared one of my favorite quotes from Amelia Mary Earhart—one that's so important to this chapter we'll come back to it again here to revisit its meaning. Yes, Amelia took to the skies for herself, but also "to have this wonderful gift produce practical results for the future of commercial flying and for the women who may want to fly tomorrow's planes."

When challenged, I remind myself that if Amelia could accomplish so much in 1937, I can surely attempt my goals today. That proof inspires me today to be a tailwind to others through my actions. It's a beautiful, cyclical pattern that will remain in motion for as long as we make the purposeful effort to *keep* it in motion. Helping one another, creating, and providing tailwinds for each other is perhaps our highest calling. At least it is for me.

Tailwinds over the South Pacific

While planning my around-the-world flight, one of my areas of focus was how to generate interest and support for the Fly with Amelia Foundation, the charity I established in 2012 for girls sixteen to eighteen seeking to earn their private pilot's license. Through social media campaigns, public events, and generous donations, we've raised more than $100,000 to date. The initial goal was simple: to create a monetary tailwind for driven young *women of tomorrow who would fly tomorrow's planes* and award each recipient a $7,500 scholarship, meant to remove the financial barrier keeping these aspiring pilots grounded.

By the time I was ready to embark on my around-the-world flight, we'd identified the first ten young women who would receive scholarships. Essays from these future female pilots arrived with deeply passionate and personal examples of how each young woman planned to make the most of her potential scholarship funds.

From the beginning, the goal of honoring Amelia Mary Earhart's legacy was nonnegotiable, which is where the delivery of the ten initial awards comes in. Rather than simply calling or send an email, I was able to announce the names of each recipient. My thinking was that, while the upcoming flight would hold at least a sliver of the world's attention, why not attempt to spotlight the future women in aviation, the future women that Amelia flew for, during a symbolic point in the flight?

So, that's exactly what I did, notifying each and every one of the young ladies via satellite text message *as I flew over Howland Island*, where Amelia and her navigator, Fred Noonan, originally intended to land. Of course, the historic team never made it to that remote and uninhabited island, but rather than focus on their disappearance, I chose this location as the point in the journey to announce our scholarship recipients.

As we circled over Howland Island, I asked my copilot, Shane Jordan, to take the controls as I sent congratulatory messages to each recipient. This emotional process filled me with excitement and nerves, pride, and hope, as I stared down at the coral island consisting of around one square mile of land 27,000 feet below.

In those brief moments above Howland Island, I felt closer to Amelia Mary than I ever had before, and I'd like to think she would have appreciated what I was attempting to do—make it just a little bit easier for other women to fly, just as she had done for me. Here I was, using today's technology, flying in a state-of-the-art aircraft, my around-the-world flight nearly complete. I had become the "woman of tomorrow" that she'd spoken of with such passion and eloquence.

Once the last message was sent, and Shane and I had soaked up as much of the meaning of this once-in-a-lifetime opportunity as we possibly could, we departed from the airspace over Howland Island. As we flew, Shane read aloud the gratitude-filled notes from future female pilots, each word acting as an affirming tailwind, making it just a little easier to keep flying toward my next destination.

Tailwinds inspiring tailwinds

Offering meaningful tailwinds requires intention and energy. It takes a concerted effort to really make a positive difference in someone else's life, to meet that person wherever she is, on her own terms, with a kind word, a thoughtful gesture, a monetary gift, or simply a compassionate, outstretched hand of love and support. Those who face the strongest, most unrelenting headwinds are in greatest need of the relief that a strong tailwind can bring.

Kamia Bradley is an extraordinary young woman in my life who knew well what it meant to face significant headwinds. From a very young age, Kamia aspired to be a pilot, but she needed a tailwind to lift her up and propel her through some very challenging circumstances. Kamia, who was fifteen years old when I met her and facing insurmountable odds and tremendous turbulence on a personal level at even that young age, showed extraordinary strength, resilience, and determination—not just to survive but to thrive . . . and to learn to fly.

We became instant friends, connecting instantly over our love of flying. Many an afternoon, Kamia and I would meet for coffee at the local Starbucks to share ideas and to talk about her dream of getting up there in the sky. Her eyes sparkling with sincere enthusiasm, she'd show up for our visits with more thoughtful insights and forward-thinking ideas than most adults would show up with for a business meeting.

After receiving a scholarship from the Fly with Amelia Foundation, Kamia completed her pilot training and is now making her mark in aviation—blazing new trails—with grace and determination. Her tremendous joy and pride in how she flies make me want to be even more like her, as she continually overcomes her obstacles and elevates herself above her circumstances to join the other women in aviation, many of whom have welcomed her with a warm, wide-open embrace. Kamia is as much a tailwind to us as we are to her.

Today, Kamia typifies that "modern woman in aviation" that Amelia Mary Earhart spoke about more than seventy years ago. This extraordinary young woman was able to achieve in a couple of months what took me eight years—obtaining her private pilot's license.

Today, she is a graduate of Embry-Riddle Aeronautical University in Prescott, Arizona, with a degree in aeronautical science, already a young leader in the world of aviation and a standout among her peers. Already generating tailwinds for other young women who will one day follow in her flight path.

That the Fly with Amelia Foundation was able to provide at least part of the tailwind that propelled Kamia toward flight makes me vitally aware of the power that we have to uplift others. Watching her soar motivates me to seek new heights in my own life. Tailwinds inspiring tailwinds.

When tailwinds come full circle

I'd like to return to this powerful paradox I talked about a little earlier in the chapter—to the unique and wonderful thing about benevolence, compassion, and the commitment to pay it forward: although these principles create forward-moving momentum, they can also be *cyclical* in nature. Returning, sometimes amplifying their impact as they're repeated, when the person who received the tailwind then creates additional momentum by becoming a tailwind herself. This is an incredible notion: that when we help others after having been helped ourselves, the very action creates both forward moving *and* cyclical momentum.

Here's a perfect example: Every year, the local chamber of commerce in Atchison, Kansas, gives out its Pioneering Achievement Award to the woman it thinks best represents the pioneering qualities of the town's most famous citizen, Amelia Mary Earhart, on behalf of the entire community. To honor Amelia's legacy and to uphold her fierce commitment to pay it forward, the chamber is paying it forward and perpetuating this positive pattern. In doing so, in creating these tailwinds, it generates both forward moving and cyclical momentum.

I was honored to receive this distinguished award in 2013, shortly before I launched my around-the-world flight. (The award itself is a beautiful bronze bust of Amelia Earhart and a $10,000 check that the recipient can donate to the charity of her choice.)

This came at about the same time the Fly with Amelia Foundation was getting off the ground, which meant that my first donation came from community leaders from her hometown. It was this donation, then, that helped me launch the charity. Again, *tailwinds inspiring tailwinds.* Women in aviation helping women in aviation. Precisely the principles Amelia believed in so passionately and urged us all to uphold.

Perhaps the most powerful underlying principle in all of this? They gave me the award *before* I launched my around-the-world flight, and as they bestowed the award upon me, they recognized me for embodying Amelia's trailblazing spirit. What was also deeply touching was their proclamation that I was receiving the award not because I was going to complete the flight but because I was going to *attempt* it.

Put simply, our *attempts* to strike out in new directions, to launch new projects, and to push ourselves past traditional

136   boundaries are what's most important. That we make the effort, put in the work, and push forward with our dreams is what counts most. And sometimes, receiving a tailwind from someone else helps push us across that finish line. Propels us toward that final leg of the journey. Helps us finish what we fought so hard to begin.

Receiving tailwinds allows us to understand what it feels like to have a little help along our journey. Bestowing tailwinds allows us to understand what it feels like to truly help another soar.

For me, that's what harnessing our tailwinds is all about.

13

DO NOT FEAR THE POINT OF NO RETURN

IN THIS CRITICAL FLIGHT LESSON, we'll humanize what I consider to be aviation's most intimidating term: *the point of no return*. This hard, fast mathematical calculation, in very simple terms, lets pilots figure out how far away from the runway they'll be when there's *no turning back*. Either you're out of fuel or you're out of an engine, but if you've flown even a few feet beyond that critical mark, you're out of luck. For Shane and me, that point came exactly eighty nautical miles from the edge of the runway at Natal International Airport, Brazil. From there, my copilot and I departed with a silent, intense focus into impossibly blue skies to complete our 7.8-hour-flight in a *single-engine aircraft* across the Atlantic Ocean.

I speak from experience when I say it takes a special kind of pilot to venture past the point of no return. This is yet another pocket of rarefied air, where you've made the intentional decision to depart over water, with no safety net.

We touched down in Natal on a Sunday afternoon as late-afternoon sunlight shone off the jet-black asphalt of the recently poured runways. I remember looking at Shane as we taxied toward the terminal with a look of "Are we even supposed to be here?" This state-of-the-art airport had been open to air traffic for less than a month, built in anticipation of the 2014 FIFA World Cup, and was a stark contrast to the thick fields of cashew trees that lined the eastern-most tip of South America. I didn't choose this airport randomly or because it was new; I chose it because it afforded us the most advantageous point of no return.

I popped open the hydraulic door of the Pilatus PC-12 and was greeted by a smiling Mr. Sabino Neto, the local aircraft salesman who was not only an expert on our specific plane and our flight but also knew a thing or two about making guests to his hometown feel welcome and immersed in the culture.

The three of us were immediate friends, sharing laughter and hangar talk on the bumpy car ride from the airport to our beachfront hotel. Sabino's energy was contagious. He didn't seem to care that we'd spent the last eight hours flying south from Trinidad and Tobago; his eagerness to hear from us firsthand about how we'd come to be on this adventure of a lifetime reminded me that life was short, and every moment should be seen as precious.

So, after checking into my room, I threw on a clean shirt and unfurled a messy ponytail. I still remember the moment

I stopped at an ornate gold mirror in the hallway to apply lipstick. In my reflection, under orange, low-wattage overhead lamps, I remember thinking that I looked and felt beautiful. This was *inner* happiness, radiating at a level that matched the colorful, vibrant environment that I'd just flown into. I skipped the lipstick.

Walking into the hotel lobby, I'm sure I smelled like a curious mix of jet fuel and perfume. We sat down to dinner at a five-star Brazilian seafood restaurant made even more captivating by the lively Sunday night crowd which included a table of three Pilatus PC-12 NG pilots. Our dinner conversation darted in every direction, overlapping mutual aviation connections and destinations we all shared in our collective logbook of flying experience.

As the restaurant emptied for the night, our conversation quieted naturally, becoming more serious. I wanted to begin discussing and reviewing the reality of the following day's flight. While our previous legs had included plenty of stretches over open water, up until this point, we had always had land to glide to or an alternate airport to which we could divert in case of emergency.

The next morning, we'd attempt to fly across the entire Atlantic Ocean, employing our wing tanks as well as our custom-designed auxiliary fuel tank, holding the precious two hundred extra gallons of fuel we'd continually rely upon during this flight. At our table, as servers bused dishes and swept the floors, we three discussed the mission, sharing our realistic fears, yes, but equally importantly, sharing our *confidence* that this was going to work. Most memorable was simply marveling at the fact that the moment had arrived: it was time to make our move.

Exhausted, encouraged, and just plain tired, I got back to my room and fell asleep immediately, in my clothes, waking up to a new kind of Monday morning stress. Shane and I met Sabino in the lobby of the hotel before sunrise with luggage, passports, overflight permits, and my mental checklists running as we casually discussed procedure for when we arrived at the plane. We'd already cleared customs, we'd fueled up for the morning, and importantly, I'd rearranged some of the contents of our plane.

During previous flights, we'd kept the life raft and open-water survival gear up against the fuel tank, several feet out of reach from either seat in the cockpit. It was heavy and we didn't want it to shift around. For *this* leg, however, I moved the life raft and the survival gear directly behind the pilot and copilot seat. They both needed to be nearby in the event of an emergency. In fact, our orange survival suits, designed to keep us somewhat warm in case of a water ditching, were already open and ready to step into if anything abnormal occurred.

To be clear, the chances of anything going wrong during our flight were next to none. Our airplane was equipped with a Pratt & Whitney PT6 engine, a turboprop engine boasting reliability and performance. Plus, the Pilatus PC-12 NG was designed with layers and layers of sophisticated technology for navigation and communication. Still, we were going to spend an entire day in the air, flying over open water, and if one thing went wrong with that one single engine, we'd have been remiss if we hadn't double- and triple-checked our plan. I'm proud of how seriously we treated this departure, and looking back I see just how much I grew as a pilot because of this challenge.

As Amelia Mary so eloquently put it, "Everyone has oceans to fly," and on that day, the "ocean" that lay before me (and below me) would be literal. In a way, I'd crossed my personal point of no return on my journey toward becoming my own version of Amelia Earhart when I decided to fight for my flight after learning I wasn't related to her. That was a flight I feel that I mostly faced solo. Today, I could rely on a strong aircraft, a smart and equally prepared copilot, and the encouragement of our new friend Sabino as he waved and cheered us along as we taxied away.

Cleared for takeoff, we approached the runway and launched into blue skies overhead. Focused, clearheaded, and confident, we ran checklists and closely monitored engine parameters. Everything was *in the green*—pilot-speak for *normal*. At a mere eighty nautical miles offshore, we'd crossed our point of no return.

Much to my surprise, the plane did not suddenly begin acting erratically or give any less than every bit of effort I asked of it as we confidently cruised at 270 knots toward the western-most tip of Africa—Dakar, Senegal. Occasionally, my imagination (and a little bit of doubt) would creep in, causing me to repeatedly ask Shane if he thought the engine "sounded a little bit funny," and rather than brush off my concern or tell me not to worry, he always stopped, listened carefully, and then we'd decide together as to whether or not there was actually cause for concern.

And here's something else: I'd asked Shane to make a pact with me. I got it in my head that I wanted to make my first real ocean crossing without the help of the autopilot. Most modern planes are equipped with autopilot capabilities, and we use them all the time, so this would be an unusual

142   choice. I simply wanted *to see if I could do it*—for me, yes, but also maybe a little for Amelia. It would be a strenuous task, from operating and speaking with air traffic controllers on muffled, high-frequency radio signals to the physical and mental demands of controlling the plane's altitude, airspeed, and heading for eight solid hours. Shane didn't question me. As tired as I got, he encouraged me to keep on going.

Hungry, exhausted, squinting to focus, the shoreline of Dakar, Senegal, came into view. After staring out at endless blue skies, we both questioned if what we saw was land or a mirage, an optical illusion along our journey to Africa. It was, in fact, land—and we entered back into our safe harbor, now within the eighty-mile range if we needed to glide to the end of the runway. Still hand-flying the airplane—Shane will vouch for me here—*I smoothly landed in the same location Amelia Mary and her navigator, Fred Noonan, landed seventy-seven years earlier.*

Taxiing toward the airport, we could see that a celebration was taking place in the distance. Women were wearing long, flowing white dresses, children were carrying colorful bouquets of flowers as tall as they were, men in suits were milling around excitedly. There was even extra security.

We almost felt like we were intruding when we were instructed to park so near to this group. Surprisingly, everyone's attention became fixated on our plane. As we opened the door this time around, we realized that this group was here to welcome us! Officials from the local airport had, without our knowledge, coordinated a surprise welcome event with our marketing team to welcome us to Africa. Tears welled up and out of my eyes as I began to fully understand how beautiful this story was becoming the more oceans I chose to cross.

The following morning, we departed Dakar at sunrise, 143 bound for Sao Tome, a tiny island off the western coast of Gabon. After takeoff, I immediately and happily engaged the autopilot, letting the airplane's computer take over as we monitored the controls for any changes. While we flew, I took time to gaze at cloud formations and ask Shane about his kids. We shared stories and simply enjoyed those precious moments together in the sky, flying toward Gabon. We'd passed our own point of no return as a crew and now as friends.

Along this leg, I snapped a photo of the two of us; a photo that's turned out to be one of my favorites from the entire trip. Shane, to my right, with a laid-back smile, and me, shiny-eyed and beaming, wearing the big magenta flowers the kids had enthusiastically pressed into my arms when they'd welcomed us so warmly to their hometown the day before.

It's your calculation to make

I want to say something else about entering a point of no return: when we announce our goals, our dreams, and our visions to others—when we actually say them *out loud*—it can often make us feel like we've "sealed a deal" that cannot be reversed or altered, as if the announcement itself has pushed us to a point of no return. We need to be careful with this.

When I announced my flight around the world, as energizing and pride-inspiring as the announcement was, I was also immediately consumed by the feeling that from that point forward, there was no turning back. No reversal of plans.

144   On an intellectual level, of course, I knew I could change my mind, back out, or modify whatever aspect of the flight I chose—this was my flight to make and my journey to define—but on an emotional level, I was worried that a change of heart or a reversal in my decision would disappoint others. Looking back, I realize just how much power this gave to others and how much unnecessary pressure and stress this placed upon me.

As you fly forward with your dreams and goals, try not to let yourself be bound and burdened by the expectation of others. Remind yourself that you *always* have options. You always have the right to decide to redirect, modify, or even walk away from that goal or that dream if, after exploring all your options, you feel like a course correction (or even a course reversal) is necessary.

Also, remember that this vision first blossomed *within you*, as an internal spark that was first ignited in your mind and in your heart. It belongs to you. Don't let external pressures define it, shape it, or influence it. Give yourself permission to change your mind. This life is yours to navigate.

One way to grant yourself the emotional space you need to change your mind (if changing your mind becomes necessary) is to develop an exit strategy in the event you should need one, a parachute in the event you need to ditch the plane entirely. Put a plan in place.

If the junior sales associate feels miserable or misused at his firm, for instance, he must create a realistic exit strategy to remove himself from the situation in a way that allows him to fly as efficiently as possible into another airspace. That could be putting aside more money from each paycheck or cutting down on his monthly expenses to grow his nest egg so that he can eventually cut the cord and walk away from this job that he hates. The point is that it is within his control, just as it is within *your* control. There are always preventive, strategic steps we can take, providing we're aware enough—and confident enough—to take them.

I will always remember the sight of that vast ocean beneath me as we traveled toward Dakar, challenging me to make it to the other side. I'll also remember the relief of spotting land, after hours of anticipation, giving me time to begin planning the next adventure.

14

HONE YOUR VISION BEYOND SIGHT

FOR THIS FLIGHT LESSON to really sink in, we need to begin by visualizing ourselves in the cockpit, sitting tall and confident in the left seat, as pilot in command, along a solo journey. Nearing the end of your flight, you spot a dense layer of clouds in your path. Within moments, visibility is down to zero, and suddenly *you are flying inside of a cloud.*

Instinctively, your focus lowers to your instrument panel; even when you can't see the airport ahead, you know these steady and reliable tools will get you there. At this level of high-stakes, sophisticated flying, you've developed what I consider to be a pilot's superpower: vision beyond sight.

To keep this superpower sharp, you must trust yourself, and you must trust your plane; it's time to allow the sophisticated instrumentation of the cockpit to function as your eyes while the clouds block your view. After a solid thirty minutes of disorienting and fatiguing flight, scanning instruments, and analyzing information, the light in the cockpit begins to shimmer as thick clouds surrender to a piercingly blue sky. You've navigated through the storm. On course. On schedule. You knew your aircraft and your flight plan so well that even when you couldn't even see it with your own eyes, you knew you'd find a safe runway on which to land.

That's vision beyond sight.

It can take pilots years to feel confident in situations like this. Spatial disorientation is real; it happens when our brain receives conflicting information about what's up and what's down. In rare cases, pilots can end up in inverted flight, completely disoriented as a result of trusting their bodily sensations rather than their aircraft. This is when crashes occur. Developing vision beyond sight is as much about *attitude* as it is about behavior: you've got to believe in and trust the process *wholeheartedly* along the way.

There's a quote I often use in my speeches and appearances that has resonated with me since my early days in flight, and I'm still drawn to it today because of its timeless, almost elegant quality and because it still makes so much practical sense. It comes from the 1942 edition of the US Navy's *Approach* magazine. I want to share that quote again here because I want to make this beautiful concept *yours, too.* I want to bring what was then an obscure quote that probably very few people fully understood into the bright light of modern day and invite it to lead us into this Flight Lesson on vision beyond sight: "Instrument flying is when your mind gets a grip on the fact that there's vision beyond sight."

Developing vision beyond sight is developing the ability to move toward your goal and arrive at your desired destination *even when you cannot see the ultimate destination in front of you.* To do this, you must have both a heightened level of inner confidence and a heightened level of self-awareness; it does require both. This is by far the top quality I admire (and look for) in others—the ability to forge a path toward an idea, a concept, *a better life,* knowing that you will find *your right path* along the way.

That's why I believe *vision beyond sight is a superpower.* Hone yours and you'll begin spotting open paths where others only see roadblocks. Creative solutions where others only see complicated problems. And if you hone this superpower correctly, you'll become an intelligent optimist, unafraid of flying into situations where immediate clarity isn't guaranteed.

All of us have tapped into our vision beyond sight in some form or fashion: I am still fully able to run a marathon without seeing the finish line, for instance. I've trained long and hard for the race. I've put in the work and I've prepared myself physically, mentally, and emotionally. I've studied the course thoroughly, and I trust myself enough to know that if I follow that course, I will arrive at my destination. Most importantly, I trust my *gut*. I know within me that this race is mine to run—and it's mine to *win* if it turns out that way, but as we learned in Flight Lesson 12 on tailwinds, the attempt is more important than the outcome. If I didn't attempt the race, the opportunity to *win* it would not even exist.

If you were to take a poll of my closest friends and ask them to describe me in a couple of words, I'm pretty sure most of them would describe me as a dreamer—someone able to creatively visualize what I want and then just as able to get up and go after it. I am deeply proud of this reputation. It's so much more than simply believing in myself; it's the intentional drive to be someone who brings visions to reality. Without it, I wouldn't have been able to conceive, plan, attempt, and complete my around-the-world flight.

A flight around the world is an *abstract* concept . . . trust me, there were no step-by-step, how-to books to turn to when the hundreds of challenges I encountered kept popping up along the way. This means there was no plan to follow, which also meant there was no wrong way to go. I knew that my inner compass would get me there, though, *even if I was the only one who could visualize it at first.*

Vision sheds light on the big picture

Consider this important nuance: developing vision beyond sight doesn't always mean you'll keep flying toward your goal. The beauty of this skill—this superpower, if you will—is that if you trust it enough and surrender to it fully, it can save you from flying into danger . . . meaning you'll learn to discern if the destination you're flying toward is truly part of your vision and adjust accordingly.

When you become the type of person who acts upon her vision beyond sight, you'll need to anticipate disappointing others when you choose to do what's right for you. Listening to your inner voice closely enough to cancel that upcoming trip, for instance, because the circumstances shifted, and the journey somehow no longer *feels* right. When something in you whispers, "This feels imbalanced. I don't trust this person. I'll be stretching myself too thin," speak up and do what allows *you* to stay in flight. Listen to yourself.

We must learn to honor those moments and listen to these voices, whether they are our own inner voices or the voices of those who stand within our trusted, experienced circle. Yes, this will sometimes necessitate a definitive course correction—from clearly asserting boundaries to sometimes removing ourselves entirely—but when we prioritize our safety and our goals, we can recalibrate our flight path and fly toward skies that support our success.

Each of our past mistakes and each of our imperfect attempts has a greater purpose. We can let our experiences and encounters from the past—the things that didn't turn out quite the way we expected or wanted or thought we needed at the time—function as a second line of vision as well. Every single entry we've made into our flight logbooks, good or bad, negative or positive, can be used to help guide us as we move toward our next goals. They can function as our second line of sight. Experience gives us clarity. Clarity lends a greater sense of direction. All of this helps us hone this superpower within us. But we have to put in the work.

Channeling calm in the chaos

In aviation, redundancy is everything. When multiple instruments present consistent information, we can fly forward with confidence. That confidence is built upon logic as well as the emotional assurance that even though all you see is a wall of dark clouds, you're still on the right track.

Let's get back in the cockpit, where we first began our chapter: during the swirling storm, our vision beyond sight remained finely tuned. We were able to rely on our airplane's sophisticated GPS system to guide us through the storm, the steady directions from air traffic control (who can see things we cannot see), and when you choose, a copilot, perhaps, to provide additional support and guidance. All these things create a second line of sight. All of them help sharpen our *own* visual acuity, and taken together, they increase the likelihood that we will make it through the storm safely to arrive at our destination.

When we break our fears down to their most basic elements, we're left with the consequences these fears represent: failing to reach our destination, getting lost along the way, or maybe even a crash landing. Finding multiple sources to verify our progress can help keep us on track and moving in the right direction: we can ask others to take a look at our plan or research others who have accomplished similar goals, making checks like these part of our planning procedures. Just as we discussed in the previous Flight Lesson on the point of no return, knowing where to focus our attention in times of stress can help keep us safe. Emergency plans sound boring until we need them. So, create yours to match your comfort level, and if you don't have one, research and create one.

Find power in your past

I want to stress that we learn from our past experiences and encounters. We can all agree that no one wants to fly through a tough storm with a pilot who has only flown in perfectly calm blue skies. Take this concept to heart; weave it into the fabric of your own daily life. Remember that your past encounters, your past experiences, are what make you *you*. Your life experiences are what will comprise your one-of-a-kind logbook that others may someday study to inspire their own ventures.

We learn from every single one of our attempts, regardless of the outcome of the journey. This is what provides ballast and direction as we fly toward our next exciting destinations, many of which we still cannot even see, but we know that they are there, waiting to welcome us. We learn from all of it. But we learn the *most* when we have given ourselves permission to trust our gut. And sometimes this may mean trusting that which we cannot see.

In my own life, whenever I'm feeling discouraged, dispirited, or a little lost and vulnerable, I turn to my past experiences to propel myself forward. I remind myself that I am better, stronger, and more trusting than the doubt or the fear of the anxiety that may be trying to invade my space. How do I do that? By turning to what I know I'm made of, and by reminding myself that the person I am today is precisely the person I want to be—confident, clear-headed, and constantly growing and evolving.

When I'm feeling *less than* or *not enough*, or when I lack the energy to simply do the work, all I must do is whisper five words to get me back on track: *I flew around the world.* These five words scribbled on a sticky note in my view as

I write this page have made a profoundly positive influence on my present, and I say the words out loud: I flew around the world. When I choose to listen to these words, to really let them settle in, they have the power to snap me into action, providing instant validation of how great it feels to make moves toward my vision.

What are your five words? Or ten words? Or *one* word? Name the moment you feel most represents the time you trusted your gut and pushed forward toward something only you could see. Use it as proof that your attitude and actions can lead to big results that you'll be proud of. Think back to the times when you trusted your gut, when you accomplished an extraordinary goal; how good it felt to have relied on your own instincts. This is where true mental, emotional, and spiritual growth can occur. No, the external world might not see this as evidence of growth, but that doesn't matter because it should be evidence enough for you.

Only you can see with perfect clarity what your ideas look like and what your goals look like. That is enough. Why? Because this is what will allow you to push them toward being real and absolute and tangible in the external world. When your goals evolve into something that others can see and feel, then something miraculous happens: your goals have moved from being quiet, internal ideas to bold, tangible *reality* that the rest of the world can see.

People still ask me, "Do you think you would have been a pilot if your name wasn't Amelia Earhart?" The honest answer is *probably not.* (My goal during my youth was to be an English teacher.) But as I began to give power to the name, and as I began to relate with the goals, dreams, and vision of Amelia Mary Earhart—regardless of whether or not I was related to her—I began to see what I hadn't been able to see before: that *this* Amelia is unique, passionate, and self-propelled, confident enough to listen to her own voice and to trust her gut in a way that pushes me toward destinations I cannot even see.

Even if I'd never pursued flight and if I'd never separated from the runway to embark on a journey that would circumnavigate the globe, I know I would have pursued something similarly spectacular. I say this not to brag or boast but because I know what I'm made of, and I want you to give yourself permission to take a good, long look inside yourself to fully discover and appreciate all that you are made of, too.

Refine this superpower within you. Sharpen your vision. Rely on *your* instrumentation and that of those you trust to help get you across that finish line. Remember you can still run the race—and *win* it, if that's how it turns out—without being able to see the finish line. Why? Because you already know that finish line is there . . . waiting for you to burst across it.

I know I've done my best if I've done as much as I possibly could to bring the ideas that circle inside my mind to life. While some attempts will blossom into wild success and others will clunk along, remembered only for their lessons learned, each will enhance my superpower of vision beyond sight—the ability to create my destination as well as the route *I choose to take* to get there.

15

BRACE FOR TURBULENCE

WHEN SMOOTH SKIES suddenly turn turbulent, all you need to do is watch the various reactions of the passengers to understand that we all react to turbulence differently.

Picture a row of passengers on a flight bound for Denver International Airport: they're all experiencing precisely the same turbulence, mind you—what differs is their *reaction* to it.

In the aisle seat, a first-time flier white knuckles the armrests of his seat, eyes darting between the "fasten seat belt" light and the face of the flight attendant as he searches for signs of alarm in her expression and questioning every "ding" with terrified sincerity. In the middle seat, a retired airline captain dozes in and out of almost sleep, arms folded comfortably across a completed newspaper crossword puzzle, his small bag neatly stowed under the seat in front of him.

Pressed up against the window, an unaccompanied minor, maybe eleven or twelve years old, smiles down at the puffy, white popcorn-shaped clouds while she fiddles with the tiny plastic wings the flight attendant has passed her way.

Muffled passenger noises quiet as the captain begins to announce that in just a few moments it will be time to start the initial descent into Denver. Before the short announcement is even finished, though, a loud "thud," a high-pitched "creak," and a few surprised gasps from the passengers overtake the sound from the speakers. The captain's tone immediately shifts from conversational to commanding: "Flight attendants, take your seats."

In this moment, on board the same flight, our three passengers are experiencing three very different reactions. In the aisle seat, our nervous flier becomes even more anxious, and as the bumps and jolts continue, the collective energy on the plane shifts from casual to high-stress—and all the pilot has shared is, "We're entering into an area of turbulence." The dozing captain in the middle seat feels those same jolts and hears those same loud, shifting creaks, but to him, bumpy skies toward the end of the flight signal he is *home*. The experienced captain knows that planes often experience turbulence near this particular airport. And the little girl in the

window seat? She just thinks, *Woo-hoo! Those bumps were fun,*
like a roller coaster! Let's go back and do it again!

While the turbulence I described in this scenario would be categorized as "light," possibly causing a few overhead items to shift and our bodies to feel slight pressure from our seat belts, this much is crystal clear: each passenger experiences it *differently*.

In our own lives on the ground, we all experience turbulence differently. Our reaction to upheaval, crisis, or even the occasional bumpy encounter is largely influenced by our past experiences, by the stories we've been told, by the knowledge we've sought out, by the homes in which we grew up—I could go on and on—but the point is that multiple factors determine our natural response to turbulence. Each person experiences it differently.

We've all lived a completely unique set of experiences, interwoven with varying levels and sources of information, forms of bias, deeply ingrained fears, preconceived definitions of love, as well as all the personal challenges we face as we simply live our daily lives. Each one of us is unique. This is why within one single row of airplane seats, the same *physical* turbulence can be experienced as panic, as comfort, and as joyful curiosity by different people.

Do not waste one single moment regretting or judging how you've responded to turbulence in the past. The past is finished, and the present awaits you. Rather than regretting how you've handled turbulence in the past, spend these precious moments in the *present*, improving your understanding of the skies you are flying in today . . . and the skies you plan to fly into tomorrow. What the scared passenger in the aisle seat didn't know was that the turbulence he'd just encountered on descent was about as serious as the small, unexpected pothole he hit last winter on his way to the grocery store: it didn't cause a *crash*, but it sure reminded him to sit up straighter at the wheel and pay closer attention to the road going forward.

When life's turbulent moments—the unexpected job loss, the sudden health scare, the financial setback—arise along your path, I urge you to take a lesson from each of our three passengers. From our fearful flier in the aisle seat, we receive a reminder that turbulence must be *understood* before we can truly be comfortable in flight. From our captain in the middle seat, we learn that knowledge and understanding of turbulence *can* allow you to relax, but during this understanding we must still never allow ourselves to become too comfortable or cocky. And from the open-minded child in the window seat, we're shown the beauty in remaining eager and ever curious.

This precise combination of attitudes is what has allowed me to clearly define the person I am today: an experienced pilot *and person*, joyfully navigating through life's ever-changing skies, never forgetting that there will always be more to learn along the way.

Types of turbulence

When we close our eyes and imagine flying through turbulence, it's easy to picture a towering thunderstorm. These are big, moisture-filled storms packed with powerful updrafts and downdrafts that can be challenging for even the most experienced pilot to navigate. When I describe life's challenges *we can see coming and therefore plan for*, that's the kind of storm I hope you picture in your mind.

For instance, once you've made the decision to go back to school while working and raising a family at the same time, you've essentially committed to navigating the challenges as they come. You know what's ahead; you can see it coming, but this knowledge about the coming turbulence affords you a freedom of sorts because you can, to some measure anyway, prepare for its arrival. Yes, the next four years will certainly hold their fair share of turbulence, but you know the bumps will be worth the reward of reaching your destination. Let's call this *turbulence confidence*.

Turbulence confidence, then, is understanding that while life's turbulence may bruise me, I won't let it knock me down for good. I can remember experiencing this kind of turbulence even as a child. If I could see a challenge coming, it didn't have a chance of surviving and blowing up into something bigger. In fact, I *lived* for and thrived upon any challenge or complicated project I could see coming, simply because I knew I could dissect it, then slowly, methodically reconstruct it in a new way that *allowed me to be creative*—whether it was designing and constructing elaborate outdoor forts as a child, or making it to the National High School Debate Championships for two consecutive years, or working multiple jobs in college to pay for my flight lessons. This is what I loved about myself as a child and what I still love about myself today: my built-in ability to brace for, live within, and fly through turbulence and challenge.

There is, however, another type of turbulence that can catch even the most experienced pilots off guard: clear air turbulence.

Before I explain this incredibly important lesson, it's *critical* you understand what makes it different from turbulence confidence.

160   Unlike the easy-to-spot, towering thunderstorm in the distance, clear air turbulence is just that: clear. It's nearly impossible to detect, and a plane that encounters clear air turbulence can experience quite a bit of damage.

This form of powerful turbulence only occurs when flying over mountains and at extremely high elevations, but it always occurs *at the point where two air masses, each moving in different directions, traveling at different speeds, collide.*

My trial by turbulence

When I learned, by way of an unexpected, on-air reveal by a newsroom colleague, that the genealogy report I'd been referencing for years was incorrect, it hit me like clear air turbulence: it was unexpected, impossible to detect, and it felt like two different air masses, moving in different directions and at different speeds, colliding.

In August of 2013, I was invited by the *Today* show to fly to New York to appear live on the show to talk about the upcoming launch of my around-the-world flight. I remember being on cloud nine (so to speak) as I walked into the studio to be interviewed by two of the female journalists I'd most admired for years, Natalie Morales and Savannah Guthrie. That day, we were also joined on the couch by Al Roker and Carson Daly.

The interview went exactly as I'd hoped it would; they all made me feel immediately at ease, and we discussed everything from the complexities of my flight plan to the goal and purpose of my Fly with Amelia Foundation, to all the ways I'd planned to honor Amelia Mary Earhart along the way. Of course, when I was asked the question of my relation to the first Amelia, I stated that we "shared a distant common ancestry, tracing back to the 1700s."

As I've shared before, up until this point, I had always quoted the results of the genealogist I'd hired in college back in 2004, which was still several years before any form of online family tree mapping would become commonplace. I'd looked the genealogist up in the Yellow Pages, knew I had only five hundred dollars to spend, and accepted her words at face value when she told me that we "shared a distant common ancestry, tracing back to the 1700s."

That became my answer. No more, no less.

After the *Today* interview, I felt so happy, so excited, so proud, and so did my family and friends. My wonderful social media cheering squad spread the story far and wide, and it felt great to have shared my plan with the entire world less than six months before I'd attempt to fly around it. As I settled into my seat on my flight back home to Denver, happy tears welled up in my eyes and I didn't even try to blot them away.

These were tears of happiness, yes, but they were also tears of pride and recognition. Finally, I was beginning to live up to this big name—*not* because of a relation to Amelia but *because I had put in the incredible amount of hard work necessary to plan an actual flight around the world.*

When I landed back in Denver, I was flooded with tweets, emails, text messages, and phone calls. While I expected them to resemble the positive feedback I'd received immediately after the *Today* appearance, I was shocked and surprised to see that these were nothing of the sort.

After my *Today* appearance aired on 9News, a colleague

162 of mine (also a self-described amateur genealogist) posted on his Twitter feed: "Apologies for the error in the story that just ran claiming our Amelia Earhart is a descendant of the famous flier. Not the case." His next tweet read, "We try to catch these things before they make air—but every now and then one gets past the keeper."

Later that day, both tweets were deleted from his Twitter accounts. It didn't matter. I was suddenly being rocked and rolled by forces that felt overwhelmingly powerful and totally out of my control. This was clear air turbulence at its strongest. In its fullest fury. And at its worst. The most debilitating, the most jarring, the most painful part of this turbulence was that I didn't see it coming.

This severe clear air turbulence came suddenly—and I had no idea why I was being tagged in tweets and messages like this—messages that came at me in a furious flutter in response to his original tweets. Messages that conveyed cruel sentiments—one hoped I would crash into the ocean and die "just like the first Amelia did." Other social media comments admonished me, telling me I "didn't deserve" to have her name and how ashamed "the real Amelia" would have been of me, trying to use her name to gain fame. There were thousands.

What I wanted to know was why he hadn't shared this information about my life, my name, my identity with me *first*? Why would he independently research my name and announce his take on Twitter? We'd worked together for years, and while I'd never call us friends, he knew exactly how to get hold of me if his intention was to simply fact-check the story.

Resilience through turbulence

In the end, my colleague was right: I am not related to Amelia Mary Earhart . . . but for a long time, I thought I was.

To conduct a proper fact-check, my managers at the TV station requested I immediately hire a professional researcher to conduct an expedited report. Through an online search (that cost $3,000 to conduct), and after several weeks of sending documents back and forth, a case manager from ProGenealogists, an official Ancestry.com research firm, found over thirty lines of the Earhart name in Pennsylvania. While my family and Amelia's were living in adjacent counties, we merely shared a last name. We were not related.

I can finally say these words, write this sentence, feel this sentiment fully, without shame, anger, or embarrassment, and it feels so liberating and empowering I'm going to say it again: I am not related to Amelia Mary Earhart, but for a long time, I thought I was. It has taken me a long time to get here, to arrive at this point where I can truly, fully *release myself* from the paralyzing grip it's had over me. Why hadn't I been able to let it fully go before now? Because *how* it was handled hurt the most deeply. However, by facing and embracing that pain in this very moment, I am letting it go right now. The pain, the guilt, the embarrassment, the anger no longer belongs to me.

For months, I'd open up my work email, social media notifications, and personal voice mail at the TV station with fear, as it was not uncommon for a stranger to deliver a detailed diatribe about all the reasons they didn't think I deserved to be a pilot or to attempt my flight. I was laughed at, mocked, jeered, called "undeserving" and "opportunistic,"

164 bullied online by fellow aviation professionals, all by people who had one thing in common: they all felt they had the right to tell me what I did and did not deserve to do with my life.

I'll be honest: During this debilitating encounter with clear air turbulence, I had real thoughts about moving away, changing my name, and just disappearing. I had no appetite, I left phone calls unanswered and voice mail unchecked, and I spent a lot of time alone, wondering what I had done to deserve any of this.

I felt such searing shame, such paralyzing guilt—not because I'd just learned I definitely wasn't related to Amelia but because I knew *I should have been the one to look closer into my relation to Amelia.* I know, now, that that's what I should have done but I simply didn't know it then.

It was never a secret that I didn't know *exactly* how I was related to Amelia; the "common ancestry" response had always been enough for me. However, looking back, I now see with clarity that I could have—*should* have—kept searching until I had a definitive answer instead of relying upon that initial report. But I didn't. That's not the way it unfolded. And that's okay.

There's a phrase I've turned to for years—whenever I feel that familiar twinge of shame sneaking into my field of view—that Oprah Winfrey quotes from her close friend and mentor, the late Dr. Maya Angelou: "Do the best you can until you know better. Then when you know better, do better." While I can't go back and change history, I can fly *forward*, always seeking (and living) truth, always standing amid my own courage and convictions, knowing full well that I can handle whatever turbulence comes my way. I feel like saying *this* again, too: if I live a life of truth, courage, and conviction, I can handle whatever unexpected storm comes my way. I am braced for the turbulence.

The 60,000-foot-tall storm

During the nine-and-a-half-hour leg of our around-the-world-flight that stretched from Singapore to Darwin, Australia, Shane and I met a monumental, 60,000-foot-tall thunderstorm, positioned directly along the course we intended to fly. This was not your run-of-the-mill storm; it felt almost apocalyptic. Not only was this storm massive, it was also stunningly beautiful, shaded with colors spanning from deep purple to florescent pink, all backlit by a sunrise over the Java Sea.

While both Shane and I had meticulously studied the weather reports and were well aware of the environment we were flying into, we were both awestruck by the sheer power of its presence; we were now face-to-face with this churning, electrified, three-dimensional monster along our path. It was one thing to plan for this storm on paper but something entirely different to meet it 27,000 feet in the air.

This was not the kind of storm we could simply fly through without consequence, and while it could have been tempting to make a 180-degree turn and fly back to the airport from which we came, that was not a choice we ever considered, not once. I was an experienced pilot, equipped with modern-day technology, with an experienced partner and copilot at my side: there was no need to run from this storm.

166   With the confidence of a pilot who knew she had every right to be there, I skillfully and intelligently course corrected. Because I *understood* what was going on inside, around, above, and below that turbulent *and temporary* environment, I knew I could fly closer to it, both extending our fuel range and maintaining our safety along the way.

Because I knew better, I flew better.

Turning toward turbulence

In the final chapter of this book, we will joyfully take flight together, allowing our creative minds to elevate above personal challenges that once seemed as daunting as that 60,000-foot-tall storm. I have shared the story of my name and how deeply it has shaped my outlook in the hope that whatever it is you've been carrying around for days, months, years, even decades, you will be able to release these burdens in the same intentional way that I have. In this release comes the acknowledgment and awareness of my own perfect imperfections. It is within these imperfections that I have come to discover true freedom. You can, too.

This final chapter will also rapidly transition between *airspace* and *headspace* as we culminate each Flight Lesson with tangible, actionable methods we can logically enact here on the ground.

It would be my honor to help you learn to love the turbulence.

16

LEARN TO LOVE THE TURBULENCE

WHILE *FALLING* IN LOVE with the parts of life that bring us comfort, joy, and security is a simple, almost reflexive task, *learning* to love something as unpredictable and downright intimidating as turbulence and turmoil takes a lifetime of continuous effort. Learning to appreciate that which encourages, sparks, and sometimes even forces major growth is the only way I've found to fly forward through this life unafraid. *Not unprepared,* but unafraid. There is a difference.

Through the previous fifteen Flight Lessons, I've shared my various lenses through which challenging situations can be viewed, and I hope you try peering through these lenses when times get tough and turbulent in your own life. In this, our sixteenth Flight Lesson, not only will I show you *why* these lenses are so critically important, I will also do my best to show you *how* to look through them and see life a little differently; how to learn to love the turbulence.

Turbulence recognizes turbulence

As I begin writing this final Flight Lesson, I have the most vibrant thing I own tied around my ponytail: a Hermès silk scarf I quite irresponsibly purchased for myself six years ago, soon after completing my around-the-world flight. *This piece of fabric is a work of art.* As I feel the fabric between my fingers, I also feel an entire story begin to unfold within the framed bands of lemon yellow, navy blue, fuchsia, and turquoise. The designer, Annie Faivre, named this piece *Zenobia Queen of Palmyra,* and Hermès began selling it in 2015.

Well, I spent something like $700 on this magnificent scarf in 2015—an uncharacteristic move for me, particularly because I didn't really have that much money to spare. (Understand that I didn't make a profit from my flight at all—that was never my goal nor my intention.) But when I saw that beautiful scarf in the window, I was drawn to it like a compass needle drawn to north, and before I even recognized what was happening, I'd walked into the store and asked the woman at the counter to please show me "that one, right there!" I was pointing at what I consider to be the first piece of real art I ever purchased for myself. While it may not have played into my conscious decision to purchase the scarf, something in me may have also remembered that Amelia Mary wore and eventually designed her own scarves during her flying career.

I didn't know anything about the designer or what its intricate pattern represented, but the colors were almost hypnotizing. The last (and only) time I'd ever seen anything so spectacular was from the cockpit of the Pilatus PC-12 during my around-the-world flight, gazing down at the impossibly blue waters of the Pacific Ocean.

Later that evening, I took the scarf out of its box, laying it out flat to admire its design. Who was Zenobia, Queen of Palmyra? One Google search of her name introduced me to the Rebel Queen of Ancient Syria, who, according to the *Ancient History Encyclopedia*, was a "great warrior-queen and clever ruler, surrounded by the wisest men of her time, and influenced painters, artists, and writers." While this alone would have been enough to inspire (and justify) my purchase, there was an even bigger gift waiting for me ahead. I continued reading to discover this: Queen Zenobia is a controversial figure in ancient history because she and her family claimed to be related to Cleopatra, which was later found to be incorrect.

It didn't stop her. According to *New World Encyclopedia*, "during her brief reign, she became perhaps the most powerful woman ever in the Roman Empire." The Getty Museum even describes her as "visionary."

That very night—the same day I purchased my breathtakingly beautiful scarf—I committed, in my own mind, to writing this book. I believe sharing openhearted accounts of the turbulence we've encountered that has rattled our wings, yet has not caused us to crash, serves as a generous invitation for others to grow more comfortable within their own turbulence. When I take a deep breath and really listen to my heart, I believe I *recognized the beauty* depicted in the Queen's turbulent life. That's how turbulence works: once you've endured it, you will learn to appreciate and value all the beautiful ways it will change your life for the better.

Stretching my wings

When I remind you that the only airplane that never experiences turbulence is the one that stays locked up inside the hangar, I want you to hear me loud and clear: taking flight *means* taking on turbulence. Do not let this deter you from your goals.

If I had canceled my flight for fear of the turbulence I'd endure during my journey, *I would have denied myself the chance to test out my own wings*. Today, I'm able to share what I know, how I grew, and how that turbulence deepened every aspect of my being—and to share it with the confidence of a pilot who has circumnavigated the globe, as a pilot and a person, now with a logbook full of imperfect flights. The fact that I have flown around this complex, complicated world we live in fills me with the confidence, courage, and commitment to keep pushing toward new heights.

Here on the ground, though life's unexpected disruptions can often keep us from taking action, we must not let them become our reason *not to act*. And here, I make a personal appeal: if you are in pursuit of a goal or a dream, *follow it*. See it through. Do not allow the things that could go wrong—the possible turbulence—keep you stuck in the hangar. Hold fast to the fact that things will *always* go wrong—setbacks and turbulence are a part of life and living—but you must build up enough confidence in yourself to chase your dreams, no matter where they lead you. They won't *always* pan out (that's part of life, too), but the fact that you pursued them is what's most important.

I want you to hear *and believe me* when I say that confidently pursuing the kind of life you want to live, *with the realistic expectation of turbulence*, is itself a source of power that will truly set you apart from the rest. When you do the hard work, when you make the conscious effort to learn as much as you can about the environment in which you're attempting to operate, extraordinary growth can occur. And when you look back, after having achieved your goal, you'll realize that all the doubts, the insecurities, and the endless "what ifs" that had been deterring you were only paper tigers—and you rendered them inert when you moved forward and went after what you wanted.

Also remember that if we only take flight on the days we're *guaranteed* blue skies, much of our life will be spent grounded.

By writing and publishing this book, I have once again placed myself in the cockpit of a flight I'm *choosing to take*, and I understand sharing my take on the world, *with the world*, opens me up to criticism. Just like the 60,000-foot storm my copilot and I intelligently course-corrected around as we braced for turbulence, there are *solutions* to even the most intimidating and complicated problems and hard-to-realize goals. However, those solutions do not arrive in a nice, neat, beautifully wrapped package. They will arrive with their own turbulence . . . and they will help you learn to love the turbulence you are experiencing.

Even—no, *especially*, in your missteps, you will grow.

172 Heroism in vulnerability

If you've seen films such as *Star Wars*, *Lord of the Rings*, or *The Lion King*, you've witnessed the common full-circle narrative of the hero's journey as defined by Joseph Campbell in *The Hero with a Thousand Faces*. In the introduction to the book he writes, "A hero ventures forth from the world of common day into a region of supernatural wonder: fabulous forces are there encountered and a decisive victory is won: the hero comes back from this mysterious adventure with the power to bestow boons on his fellow man."

Put simply, we must *venture away* from the home we know and encounter turbulence, to finally return home with the specific lessons learned along the journey. And upon our return, we will inspire, motivate, and enlighten others by sharing our experiences. This kind of sharing is itself another form of heroism.

Stories that follow the structure of the hero's journey tend to resonate with us deeply, and for good reason. I believe this is because within all of us there exists the deep and fundamental understanding that turbulence truly is part of the journey, and while life would be a lot simpler without it, it's our job in this lifetime to *unearth, embrace, and befriend* this knowledge. When we think of our own life as our own hero's journey, we can even come to appreciate those who stand in our way.

My internal confidence became much stronger when I realized the immediacy with which conflict and misunderstandings could be dissolved by simply letting my guard down. Once I incorporated *vulnerability into my defense* against those who stood in my path, I became *unstoppable*.

In the traditional male interpretation of the hero's journey, vulnerability is present, but let me save you some energy: staying open, humble, and willing to learn and improve, especially when up against your greatest enemies, makes it next to impossible for them to keep fighting.

This understanding gave me real hope in the midst of my most intense turbulence, specifically as I navigated the epic storm surrounding my name. Rather than fighting to prove why I was right and someone else was wrong, I was able to respond to my critics with my heart. When I spoke from the heart and made my intentions clear, I was able to keep my flight from falling apart. Through every moment of that turbulence, every partner and sponsor of my around-the-world flight remained by my side. They never wavered. This bolstered me up with the confidence I needed to complete a successful flight around the world.

I hope this book can provide comfort and reassurance to you as you fly through your own life's turbulence, and that while you may return home as a completely different person, you'll learn to admire that person in a way that you never realized would be possible. This kind of growth is experiential; you won't feel it unfold within you until you've stood in its midst. Trust me: without the turbulence, the roadblocks, the unexpected rule changes, and the plain old hard-to-handle times when life simply isn't fair, we'd be left with a whole bunch of boring stories where everyone gets it exactly right on their first try. Where is the growth in that?

I hope you see clearly, within each metaphor, story, and lesson I've shared, that you are equipped with the very same tools for overcoming, and *how you choose to use them will be the mark you leave on this world*. Whether you're about to embark on your grandest journey or whether you're tackling a quiet, personal challenge the outside world will never see, how you choose to respond to those challenges is completely up to you.

Simple, but not easy

Across the entire globe, the longest stretch of over-water flight (no islands to land on, no airports to divert to) is between Hawaii and the U.S. mainland, making it a fitting and challenging way to bring this monumental flight plan to a close. This is precisely why my copilot and I chose this path—and because of our fuel tank modification, we became the *first* pilots of a Pilatus PC-12 NG to ever arrive in Honolulu after departing from the South Pacific. And the following day, we departed as the *first* PC-12 crew to fly to California. This leg of open-water flight on our particular flight plan was 2,093 nautical miles long, which meant we would be in flight close to eight and a half hours straight.

As I mentioned in the Introduction, I made the intentional decision to align each of the sixteen Flight Lessons in this book with the sixteen legs of my around-the-world flight. Just as each stretch of my aviation journey needed to be planned and crafted with specific intention, so, too, was each lesson I've shared with you here.

As I wrote this book, the complexity of the challenges we faced during the flight as well as the entire, wide-ranging spectrum of my emotions during the flight surfaced again. The very real fear of crossing oceans with only one engine on our plane. The fear I'd be rejected by everyone after learning I wasn't related to Amelia. The fear that my true intentions surrounding the flight would be misunderstood. I sat with *all* of those fears as they resurfaced in the writing of this book, which was itself yet another growth experience for me. So, as I've written this book, I, too, have grown. Matured. Expanded. Deepened. This is how growth occurs, not just by living within the experiences, but by *remembering* the experiences, as I did while I wrote. I accept both forms of growth as the profound gifts that they are.

More than anything, I hope this book clears you for takeoff toward the joy that can be achieved once we simply—*not easily, but simply*—learn to love the turbulence.

Open hearts over open water

On the afternoon of July 10, 2014, I landed the Pilatus PC-12 back on American soil, at the Honolulu International Airport. Shane and I were exhausted, both mentally and physically, after our trek across the South Pacific that had begun on Christmas Island that morning. While we still had an incredibly difficult feat ahead of us the following day, *flying a single-engine aircraft across the entire Pacific Ocean*, reaching this point in the journey felt like the beginning of our return home.

One of my favorite memories from the entire trip was born that evening as Shane and I each enjoyed a giant cheeseburger and fries on the patio of The Royal Hawaiian, the same hotel where Amelia Mary stayed in 1935. After dinner, we wandered through the colorfully decorated hotel, discussing details of the next day's big flight, all while walking among the black-and-white photo displays of Amelia and her navigator, Fred Noonan, on their visit to the same location.

176   The next morning, I woke up feeling rested, calm, and focused. The mission was clear: it was time to finish what we started, closing the loop on our circumnavigation of the globe.

Over the next eight hours, my copilot and I completed our flight from Honolulu, Hawaii, to Oakland, California, the Golden Gate Bridge serving as a long-awaited landmark and beautiful beacon, letting us know we were nearly home. As we approached, not only did the San Francisco approach controllers allow us to fly into their airspace right over the bridge itself, they also allowed us to approach the Oakland Airport in a way that allowed the crowd waiting for us on the ground to watch our approach to land in full view.

In the last few moments of our flight, I could tell, even without many words, that Shane and I were both letting the emotion of our flight really sink in, and this is a moment I will always keep in a special place in my heart. The moment was filled with trust, partnership, experience, and mutual respect for the all the beautiful ways we had *conquered turbulence together*. Just seconds before I landed the plane, tail number N58NG, or as I affectionately named her, the *Silver Lining*, we both agreed that *this landing* was for Amelia. And it was a smooth one.

Standing in front of the large crowd of friends, sponsors, team members, and complete strangers that had gathered to watch us land in Oakland, were my mom and my dad. As I opened the door of the aircraft, I burst into tears, my mom running excitedly toward me with a huge hug. Next, my dad gripped me tight, his calloused hands shaking as he told me how worried he was while I was gone.

In that moment, I could feel the three of us release some of the fear and pressure that we had all experienced through

the journey of navigating this name, both separately and together as a family. They were proud of me, but I was also
proud of them, proud of them for *taking the chance* to gift
me a name that had so much potential for turbulence . . . because it has been within this turbulence where I have grown
the most.

Live your life

Now that we've come full circle on my flight around the
world, I trust that you, my dear reader, now fully understand
that this book was not written to simply document each step
and experience of my life. That was *some* of it, of course, but
the larger goal was to share the beauty of these turbulent
moments in a way that can be explored, studied, and learned
from as proof that even when it *feels like* the whole world ex-
pects us to crash, we are still equipped with countless ways
to navigate the storms we face. Even as we fly toward the
turbulence, we still have choices. All it takes to create yet another path, and another, and even another, is the ability to
explore *all directions of your compass.*

When we board any airplane, we assume the risk of turbulence, yet we board the flight anyway. We know there's a
chance we'll get stuck in a holding pattern, yet we board the
flight anyway. Live your life this way by clearing yourself for
takeoff! The airplanes that endure turbulence still make it
safely to their destinations; the only thing that's different is
the pilot: *she's now better.*

You, too, will become a better person because of the
turbulence life brings, so try to apply each of these Flight
Lessons I've shared in a way that makes sense in your own

178   life. Create a journey that you're proud of. *This is what it truly means to become pilot in command of your own journey.* Do not let the world decide how much turbulence it will take to knock you down; instead, show the world, through your actions and your integrity, just how much you can handle. You can handle a lot, because life, like the sky, is in a constant state of flux, at times offering helpful tailwinds, while at others, pressing back with forceful headwinds.

Don't get me wrong, turbulence can be terrifying and yes, there are *extreme cases* where things simply get too rough to handle and we simply must quit. *That's why we have emergency procedures.* I flew around the world with a life raft and a survival kit, and I learned how to use them! I was prepared for the possibility of catastrophe, and while I didn't need to employ any emergency procedures, thank goodness, simply *knowing that I knew what to do* kept me confident in flight.

So now I ask you, what will you pack in *your* survival kit? Whatever it is, carry it always in your mind, in your heart, in *your backpack*, wherever you can access it quickly and in a way that allows you to live your life with confidence rather than with fear or doubt. For some, that's a savings account and a detailed strategic plan; for others, it's the option to move back home if a new business venture fails; while for others, it's simply their ability to swim safely back to shore. The point is you should carry with you whatever it takes to make you feel safe and supported enough to take life's biggest risks. Don't let others tell you how much security you should or should not have along the way. Only you can make that decision.

Also, be aware of who and what you bring along with you on your journey. Some of your flights will be solo; these flights will serve as a space for you and you alone to face the elements along your path and to contemplate them. There will be immense value in these trips, but do not let your solo ventures become your sole source of growth and expansion. I have learned far more from my copilots, both in the air and on the ground. Indeed, the copilots I've had in my life have supported me emotionally, including my mentors (even those I've never met) and those who have come before me, especially Amelia Mary Earhart. As you prepare for your journey, build a strong flight crew, that knows the power and potential in ground effect, and involve everyone in your passage. They will be the ones awaiting *your* return when your journey eventually comes full circle.

The parallels between taking flight and truly living also extend to how we fly. Be aware of and strict about what you choose to carry with you; this is your unique weight and balance calculation. Ask yourself, would I be able to fly more efficiently by taking inventory of *who and what* is on board my plane? These are boundaries and *you are allowed* to enforce them with as much vigilance as a pilot taking flight.

Above all, I hope you hone and trust your vision beyond sight. Your instruments are already finely tuned to provide feedback and guidance surrounding your unique abilities and needs, so trust them. When your gut tells you that you need more time to make a decision or to execute an act, *ask for that time*; when your gut is telling you that your path feels a bit off course, investigate it.

Let the hangar be the place where you rest for your next adventure, not where you attempt to preserve and protect an unscathed life.

So, take flight, *feel* those bumps, and *know* in your heart that turbulence is *proof* that you must make the all-important decision to take flight. For me, that has made all the difference.

I hope that this book has been as much of a revealing and motivating journey for you to read as it has been for me to write. Yes, we've traveled the sixteen legs of my around-the-world flight together. And yes, we've delved into sixteen important Flight Lessons that will hopefully help you experience life more fully. And yes, our collective journey has come to an end—and I feel so fortunate that we've taken it together—but the *real* journey has only just begun.

The journey that stands before you now is yours to take.

Learn to love every single minute of it . . . even—no, *especially*—the turbulence.

AMELIA ROSE EARHART holds her private, instrument and commercial ratings as a pilot, and in 2014, became an around-the-world pilot, completing a complex, one-of-a-kind flight plan inspired by her hero and namesake, Amelia Mary Earhart. Earhart partnered with Pilatus Aircraft to fly the Pilatus PC-12 NG single-engine airplane around an equatorial route, inspired by the original flight attempt of Amelia Mary Earhart and Fred Noonan in 1937.

From 2012 to 2022, Earhart ran the Fly With Amelia Foundation, granting flight training scholarships to young women ages sixteen to eighteen, across the U.S. In 2023, the Fly With Amelia Foundation donated all remaining funds to the Amelia Earhart Hangar Museum in Atchison, Kansas, Amelia Mary Earhart's home town.

A former breaking news and traffic reporter in Denver and Los Angeles, Earhart now combines her passion for flying and communicating as an international keynote speaker. To book her as a keynote speaker or guest, request an interview, and for all other media inquiries, please email AmeliaRoseEarhart@gmail.com. You can also follow Earhart on Instagram at @AmeliaRoseEarhart.

KRISTIN CLARK TAYLOR is an award-winning author, editor, and journalist. She is a founding member of *USA Today's* original creation and launch team, and serves on the newspaper's Board of Contributing Editors. She served as White House Director of Media Relations under President George H.W. Bush. She is an ordained minister and a mindfulness practitioner. Kristin can be reached at Kristintay@aol.com.

Made in the USA
Middletown, DE
18 July 2023